HEALTHY COOKING & NUTRITION FOR COLLEGE STUDENTS

How Not to Gain the Freshman 15

By Rebekah Sack

Foreword by: Jen Garcia, MS, LMHC

Healthy Cooking & Nutrition for College Students:
How Not to Gain the Freshman 15

1405 SW 6th Ave. • Ocala, Florida 34471 • 800-814-1132 • 352-622-1875–Fax
Web site: www.atlantic-pub.com • E-mail: sales@atlantic-pub.com
SAN Number: 268-1250

Library of Congress Cataloging-in-Publication Data

Names: Sack, Rebekah, 1994- author.
Title: Healthy cooking & nutrition for college students : how not to gain the
    freshman 15 / by Rebekah Sack.
Other titles: Healthy cooking and nutrition for college students
Description: Ocala, Florida : Atlantic Publishing Group, Inc., [2016] |
    Includes bibliographical references and index.
Identifiers: LCCN 2016020336| ISBN 9781620231593 (alk. paper) | ISBN
    162023159X (alk. paper) | ISBN 9781620231609 (E-ISBN)
Subjects: LCSH: College students--Nutrition. | College students--Health and
    hygiene.
Classification: LCC RA777.3 .S23 2016 | DDC 613/.0434--dc23 LC record available at https://
lccn.loc.gov/2016020336

PROJECT MANAGER: Rebekah Sack • rsack@atlantic-pub.com
ASSISTANT EDITOR: Yvonne Bertovich • yvonne.bertovich34@gmail.com
COVER DESIGN: Meg Buchner • megadesn@mchsi.com
BOOK PRODUCTION DESIGN: T.L. Price • design@tlpricefreelance.com

Printed in the United States

Reduce. Reuse.
RECYCLE.

A decade ago, Atlantic Publishing signed the Green Press Initiative. These guidelines promote environmentally friendly practices, such as using recycled stock and vegetable-based inks, avoiding waste, choosing energy-efficient resources, and promoting a no-pulping policy. We now use 100-percent recycled stock on all our books. The results: in one year, switching to post-consumer recycled stock saved 24 mature trees, 5,000 gallons of water, the equivalent of the total energy used for one home in a year, and the equivalent of the greenhouse gases from one car driven for a year.

Over the years, we have adopted a number of dogs from rescues and shelters. First there was Bear and after he passed, Ginger and Scout. Now, we have Kira, another rescue. They have brought immense joy and love not just into our lives, but into the lives of all who met them.

We want you to know a portion of the profits of this book will be donated in Bear, Ginger and Scout's memory to local animal shelters, parks, conservation organizations, and other individuals and nonprofit organizations in need of assistance.

*— **Douglas & Sherri Brown,***
President & Vice-President of Atlantic Publishing

TABLE OF CONTENTS

————0-0-0————

FOREWORD

-0-0-0-

I didn't gain the "Freshman 15." I gained what I call the "Junior 30." Yikes! Of course, there were a number of variables that resulted in this weight gain, but if I had had a friendly, knowledgeable guide along the way, maybe it would not have happened.

Now, more than a decade after college, I work with young people as a mental health counselor. On a weekly basis, discussions of diet and exercise occur. Unfortunately, some parents and caretakers are not healthy themselves and our school systems often lack well-rounded health education. The Internet is full of so much information and it can be overwhelming, not to mention misleading. Where are we to turn? *Healthy Cooking and Nutrition for College Students: How Not to Gain the Freshman 15* is a remarkable resource.

Healthy Cooking and Nutrition covers multiple aspects of physical health rather than focusing on just one. If you need or want additional information, the author, Rebekah Sack, provides an exhaustive list of references and research material. *Healthy Cooking and Nutrition* includes topics on food and exercise, yes, but it also delves into the ever-important question "what is health?" and "what does it mean to be healthy?" More than that, the book explains popular diets — all those infomercials and ads we are inundated with every day, the ones with the so-called "before" and "after" photos — Rebekah breaks them down for us in a single chapter. She gives suggestions about how to eat on a budget because, well, being broke in college is pretty much a given, and she explores the world of organic foods (what does that word even mean?). Rebekah takes the time to discuss a nutritional label and how to understand it, going so far as to share details about nutritional elements such as vitamins and minerals. Did you know there are eight different B vitamins? And that we need each and every one of them for our bodies to remain healthy? Additionally, *Healthy Cooking and Nutrition* presents practical suggestions on how to manage meal prep and cooking basics. You will never look at crock-pots the same again! Lastly, Rebekah dedicates an entire chapter to alcohol — a rather misunderstood, though popular, part of college culture today.

Rebekah does not pretend to be the ultimate authority on all things health. Rather, she shares from her own understanding, bridging the gap between everyday life and the larger realm of data and statistics. Instead of telling us what to do, Rebekah explains all our options. *Healthy Cooking and Nutrition* empowers us to make our own decisions about health, food, and body. Additionally, Rebekah doesn't tell us what our bodies should look like. Our culture is preoccupied with body size, shape, and the number on the scale. This obsession can lead to significant mental health disorders such as anorexia, bulimia, binge-eating, and body dysmorphic disorder.

While many people experience episodes of disordered eating, more serious cases result in severely impaired functioning in multiple life arenas. In fact, the National Eating Disorders Association confirms that after 50 years of research on anorexia nervosa, of all mental health disorders, it has the highest mortality rate. Not only are these statistics real and scary, it is something I know on a deeply personal level and something I see on a regular basis professionally. Rebekah helps combat this obsession with scientific truth and real-world experience. *Healthy*

Cooking and Nutrition is not trying to sell us anything — except maybe a little more self-love.

Yes, we want to stay fit and "look good" in the clothes we wear. Perhaps more importantly, we also need to recognize that our physical health is deeply connected to our mental and emotional health. *Healthy Cooking and Nutrition* is a preventative measure not just for physical health in college, but for physical and emotional health throughout adulthood.

We often hear the phrase "we are what we eat." We are also so much more. Our physical bodies deserve care and attention just as much as our emotional and spiritual selves. *Healthy Cooking and Nutrition for College Students: How Not to Gain the Freshman 15* helps to do just that through well-rounded educational information that allows us to make informed decisions about our health. Not only will I be reading this book as an adult and implementing its strategies, but I will also be using it as a therapeutic resource with my high school and college-aged clients. Reward yourself by using *Healthy Cooking and Nutrition* for not only your college years but long after.

Happy reading and healthy living!

—Jen Garcia, MS, LMHC

Jen Garcia is a licensed mental health counselor in the state of Massachusetts. She has lived and worked in Boston, MA and the greater metro area for over a decade. A graduate from Northeastern University with a Master's of Science in Counseling Psychology, Jen is most passionate about her counseling work at a Boston Public High School. There she sees kids who struggle with depression, anxiety and eating disorders as well post-traumatic stress and attachment disorders.

INTRODUCTION

We've all seen the commercials, haven't we?

"You can lose 30 pounds without changing your eating habits or adding an exercise routine! Sounds too good to be true, right? I thought so too, until I tried it for myself."

Here's another one: "Millions of Americans have lost weight with our diet pill. Join the bandwagon today!"

You see pictures of extremely obese people on the left and their slimmed down selves on the right. You might notice that there's this tiny white print on the bottom of the screen, but the pictures shift so quickly that you don't quite make out what it says.

Well, here's an eye opener. That invisible text says things like the following (these are all real commercials, but the brand names are being left out for legal purposes):

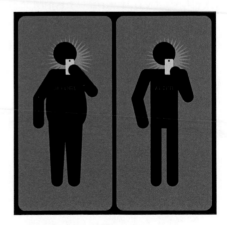

- The commercial brags about how many people have lost weight with this particular diet pill, and at the bottom of the screen, we see that about 60 percent of the people actually finished the trial: "1,436 participants out of 2,436 completed the six month clinical trial."

- The commercial brags about not having to change your current diet or establish an exercise routine — "just use this supplement!" — but their before and after example has this fine print at the bottom of the screen: "Joey used this product for 12 months with sensible diet and exercise regimen." I think it's safe to say that anyone will lose weight if they eat well and exercise for a year, right?

- How about this diet pill commercial, which says in the fine print: "[Participant's] results were achieved in combination with diet and exercise. Results not typical."

It's very possible that these diet pills and supplements do help you to lose weight, but the bottom line is, they only seem to work when you eat consciously and exercise regularly. After all, what exactly does "sensible diet" mean?

Well, that's our aim. This book isn't going to give you any get-skinny-fast claims. The goal of this book is prevention. You can also expect to see case studies from professionals sprinkled throughout the book for boosts of expert experience and advice.

You're getting ready to start your college career — your independent life is just beginning. It's so easy to get stuck in the spiral of 20 page research papers, dining center food (mac and cheese for the win), partying, and even a part-time job on the side, that we can lose sight of our health.

If you're getting ready to go to college, or if you've started college and want to get on the right track, this book is your definitive guide to success. Even if you're just curious about what exactly healthy is — is the food pyramid legitimate or is it just a government scheme? — this book has all the answers. Experts back up everything between these covers through authentic research.

There is no single answer to "healthy." You aren't going to finish this book and feel like you've been beaten over the head with a single lifestyle option. There are plenty of options out there, from types of food to types of diets. What this book is going to give you is unbiased information.

Is the vegan lifestyle for you? Flip to Chapter 3 to see the pros and cons. What exactly does the "organic" label on my groceries mean? Flip to Chapter 5 to find out. Knowing what you're putting in your body is the most important thing you can learn for yourself. I promise you — once you fully understand what's in the food you're eating, you'll make more informed decisions about what you consume, which will lead you to a healthier, more fulfilling life.

If you're thinking something along the lines of "who cares?" you're not alone. It's hard to concern yourself with preventing cancer or diabetes right now — it's not even on your radar. Instead, focus on what a healthy lifestyle can do for you *right now* (looking great in a bikini or speedo and being sharper during exam week).

Now that we've got that down, let's work on dodging the looming freshman 15.

What's the Freshman 15?

Odds are you've probably heard of this magical phrase. What exactly is it, where did it come from, and why is it such a popular thing? Let's break it down.

This phrase originated in 1985, making its first appearance in the Chicago Tribune. It's a catchy phrase, and it's the idea that during your first year of college, you're prone to gaining about 15 pounds. The lifestyle change and bad eating habits all come together to put you in a dark, weight-gaining spot.

The funny thing is, this kind of came out of nowhere. There's no research indicating that you'll gain 15 pounds as a freshman. Studies show that it's actually closer to seven or eight pounds, but how catchy does "The Freshman 8" sound?

While the weight-gaining problem isn't as out-of-control as everything thinks, it's still a problem. USA Today published an article in 2006 explaining the results of studies done on this epidemic. Here's what researchers at Brown found when they did a study on almost 1,000 students.

- Students at Purdue gained about 7.8 pounds, mostly within the first semester.
- By the end of their sophomore year, the students gained about two more pounds, making the grand total somewhere between 9-10 pounds.

So, why is this happening? Why does the sudden shift from life at home to life on campus cause such a drastic change in health? Well, Nanci

Hellmich, the writer of this article, interviewed several freshmen to figure it out.

One student explains that it's the ability to eat whatever you want, whenever you want. In other words, there's no mom or dad over your shoulder scolding you for eating cold pizza for breakfast.

Another problem is the dining hall. Almost all freshmen are required or are offered to have a meal plan when they first go to college: "Nobody at home is cooking like a dining hall. They don't have five different entrees and five different desserts at home," says Leslie Bonci, a sports nutritionist (Hellmich).

When you sign up for college, you generally pay a flat fee for this dining hall buffet, so you feel the need to eat as much as you can to get the best bang for your buck. After all, the meal plans are stinkin' expensive.

So, here we are, eight pounds later, and we're visiting home for Thanksgiving. Eunice Eun, a sophomore in college, explains to Hellmich, "It was really startling for my parents when I went back home for Thanksgiving break."

You parents aren't used to your plumper self, and chances are, you're not feeling the best either. Eating junk food for breakfast, lunch, and dinner isn't just causing you to gain weight. It's dragging you down, making it harder to focus, and it's giving you constant headaches.

Here's the problem — how are we going to fix it? Most people would say something like, "go on a diet." That sounds like a promising idea, but maybe it's not the best answer.

Dieting vs. Lifestyle

The classic, American foodie lifestyle includes the following: eat processed, cheap food for a long time, gain weight, be subjected to various weight-related diseases (it's inevitable), become reliant on loads of prescription drugs to treat the issues related to the weight gain, and die.

It sounds so horrible, yet it's so true. Joe Fuhrman, author of "The End of Dieting: How to Live for Life," abbreviated the phrase "standard American diet" to SAD. How convenient.

So, generally, when someone says they're going on a diet, they step away from the SAD and rely on some kind of previously established plan, whether it be the Atkins diet, Weight Watchers, Nutrisystem, or some other idea of what healthy should be, which a lot of time means cutting down drastically on calories.

They do this "diet" until they reach their goal, and then they go back to the SAD. We can all see where this goes wrong, right? Gaining the weight back is unavoidable. NBC News reports on a study done by researchers at the University of California at Los Angeles (2010): "about two-thirds of dieters regained more weight within four or five years than they initially lost."

Basically, dieting is a huge fail. The mindset and execution is all wrong. How do we sidestep the failed idea of dieting, yet still manage to eat things that taste good… forever?

This brings us back to Fuhrman and his book "The End of Dieting." The reason people go on diets is to lose the weight they've managed to gain. They think something along the lines of, "I can handle eating this diet food for a short amount of time," so that's what they do. We're so conditioned to like foods that are high in sugar — even our bread has tons of sugar in it — that when we starve ourselves from it, we're unhappy with the taste.

It's almost like we're addicted to sugar or something (cough, cough).

Fuhrman gives us hope: "A high-nutrient diet will reduce your desire for high-calorie, low-nutrient foods." Think potato chips and ice cream. He continues, "Within weeks, your taste buds will change, and you'll lose interest in the unhealthy foods you once thought you could never live without."

You saw that right — your taste buds will change.

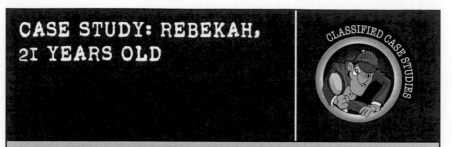

CASE STUDY: REBEKAH, 2I YEARS OLD

I used to drink coffee — the loaded-up-with-cream-and-sugar-and-flavoring kind of coffee. The mere taste of black coffee caused my nose to scrunch up. The bitterness made me gag.

I decided to put myself on a mission — the mission of weaning myself off of sugar in my coffee. Every time I drank coffee, I'd add a little less *stuff*. Over the course of about a year, I found myself preferring black coffee.

Now, when I taste coffee with loads of cream and sugar in it, I don't like it at all — it's far too sweet. I, personally, have experienced this phenomenon of shifting taste buds.

You may be thinking *yeah right*, but if you stay vigilant with your healthy lifestyle, you'll realize that you crave those healthful foods, and you'll soon be repulsed by the processed junk food you've come to love.

In the words of Fuhrman, "Anything you adopt temporarily only begets temporary results, and fluctuating your weight up and down is not lifespan favorable."

If you want to look better, and more importantly, *feel* better, then you need to focus on changing your lifestyle, which is permanent.

CHAPTER 1

-O-O-O-

Why Eat Healthy?

If you're still not sure about all of this, let's take a look at why eating healthy matters. It can be difficult to think about your health when college is taking over your life. It's hard enough to get any sleep at night, let alone make it to class without pajamas on.

If you're looking for someone to give you that extra kick in the behind, here it is.

Risks

Let's say you continue on this ramen noodle, boxed cereal, pop tart, and chocolate chip cookie dough ice cream before bed diet, and you don't plan on stopping any time soon. What will happen to you?

Cancer

There's this common idea that cancer is inevitable. There's nothing you can do to get away from it — it's coming for you. Many people think that this is how they will die. There's no cure, only painful treatments, and we all know a variety of people that either have it now or that have passed away from its painful grip.

"The China Study" by Thomas and T. Collin Campbell (2006) reports many current health studies and their findings. According to The American Cancer Society, men have a 47 percent chance of getting cancer, and females have a 38 percent chance. Americans have the highest rate of cancer in the entire world.

Studies reveal the link between cancer and obesity; this research started in 2003. The Department of Nutritional Sciences at the University of Texas at Austin published research that explores the link between obesity and prostate cancer (2014).

It's not that being obese causes prostate cancer, it's that the effects of obesity increase added problems, such as death: "Increasing evidence suggests that high adiposity, body mass index, and waist circumference are positively correlated with higher grade Gleason scores (6), higher rates of biochemical recurrence, and a 50% increase in prostate cancer mortality" (Cavazos).

In other words, when you have extra fat on your body, it worsens your existing condition, making it twice as likely that you'll die if you have prostate cancer.

And that's just one study.

Another study (2013) explains that if you aren't physically active, you're more likely to develop breast cancer (Guinan). This study also finds a correlation between obesity and death by cancer: "Obesity at diagnosis is associated with poorer survival and increased breast cancer recurrence."

If you're still skeptical, the third time's the charm.

According to the International Agency for Research into Cancer (2015), about 20 percent of cancer cases are a result of the patient being obese. This is mainly due to excess fat in the body as well as a lack of exercise (Surmacz). The American Association for Cancer Research reports that overweight/obesity is the cause of about 25 percent of cancer cases (Obesity Society).

No matter how you slice it and dice it, the link is clear. While it's still entirely possible to get cancer if you're at a healthy weight, it's less likely.

No one wants to be sitting across from a doctor, preparing to hear the news of "I'm so sorry, but you have cancer" — especially if it can be prevented through a healthy lifestyle.

Diabetes

Cancer sounds bad enough, but when you throw diabetes into the mix, the weight of an unhealthy lifestyle starts to grow. Diabetes can cause the following problems for you: chronic hyperglycemia, blindness, kidney disease, and amputations. You're also two to four times more likely to have a stroke. Diabetes is one of the leading causes of death in the U.S.

Being overweight is not the only reason people are diagnosed with diabetes, but according to the Obesity Society (2015), about 90 percent of people living with type II diabetes are overweight. When you're overweight, there's extra pressure on your body's ability to use insulin, which makes it more likely that you'll develop this disease.

The No. 1 way to prevent or delay diabetes? Studies have shown that "lifestyle changes and small amounts of weight loss" do the trick (Obesity Society). Keep in mind that it's not dieting or short bursts of healthful living — it's the lifestyle change that makes the difference.

CASE STUDY: ANATOLY BELILOVSKY, M.D.

Belilovsky Pediatrics
Brooklyn, New York
www.babydr.us

Dr. Anatoly Belilovsky treats college students in his pediatrics practice. When asked what problems he is seeing in his college-aged patients due to a poor diet, he commented:

"As with most overweight patients, diabetes is always a risk with poor diet and a sedentary life style. More basic effects of poor diet include increased fatigue, lowered brain function, and digestive irregularities. Mental health is also affected by weight gain due to a changing self-image and self-worth. Many times, students use food and alcohol to cope with new emotions over sudden independence, unfamiliar environments, and social situations. This, coupled with weight gain, can lead to depression, anxiety, and eating disorders."

He feels that students should make it a habit to get up 30 minutes earlier each day in order to go for a workout or take a brisk walk around campus. Belilovsky advises students to make a point of putting more octane in their engines with more nutritious foods. His top advice to students includes:

1. Do not eat while doing something else (e.g., reading, writing, computer, TV). Eating should be mindful so you actually pay attention to what foods (calories) are entering your body and when you are full. This will cut down on excessive eating and the potential to gain weight through empty calories.

2. Do not drink your calories. Drink water, and plenty of it. No juices (eat the whole fruit or vegetable from which juice is made), no sugary/corn syrupy sodas, and limit alcohol consumption to reduce major empty calories that cause you to overeat and gain weight.

3. Choose fat-free versions of whatever you like to eat. Less caloric density means that even if you cannot control binge eating (like late at night), there are only so many calories that will fit in.

Anatoly Belilovsky, M.D., has been a board-certified pediatrician since 1990. He is the medical director of Belilovsky Pediatrics in Brooklyn, New York. Belilovsky is a clinical instructor in pediatrics at the Weill College of Medicine and is the recipient of an Americhoice Quality of Care Award. He has a blog at www.babydr.us.

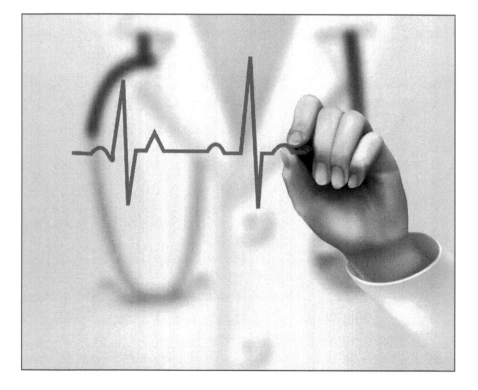

Heart disease and stroke

When blood can't properly get to your heart, you will suffer from really uncomfortable chest pains, and it's possible that a heart attack or heart failure is in your future.

If you're carrying tons of extra fat around (and we don't mean a bag of olive oil), plaque — a waxy substance — starts to build up around these arteries that are around your heart. That plaque makes it impossible for your heart to get the right amount of blood.

Not only will you suffer from heart disease, but you can be subject to a stroke, because that plaque buildup can cause a blood clot.

Another way for you to get heart disease is through unhealthy amounts of blood fats being in your body. When your triglycerides are too high, and your ratio of good cholesterol and bad cholesterol is off, you're at a higher risk for heart disease.

The American Heart Association (AHA), the Obesity Action Coalition, and a plethora of researchers have recognized the direct correlation between overweight/obesity and heart problems — this is not a myth.

General discomfort, from sleep to joint problems

Imagine walking around every single day with 15 pounds of books in your arms. Maybe that's not so hard to imagine. You are not allowed to set them down. You'd probably be a little uncomfortable, and maybe even a little sore.

Now, imagine carrying around a 50-pound backpack, and for years at a time. It will do damage to your body, specifically to your joints.

That's exactly what being overweight/obese feels like for people. It's almost like they're carrying around another human being on their back — sure, their leg muscles have gained strength by carrying around all of that extra weight, but not enough to stop their bodies from the discomfort of all the extra fat.

Those extra pounds can cause osteoporosis, a joint problem that concerns knees, backs, and hips. The extra weight causes extra pressure, which starts to break apart the protective tissue around the joints.

Another common problem for people who are significantly weighed down is sleep apnea. This is when you actually stop breathing during the night for short periods at a time. When there's a lot of fat around your neck, it puts a lot of pressure on your airway, causing it to close up.

If all of these life-threatening issues weren't bad enough, throw in the other discomforts, such as gallstones, infertility, metabolic syndrome, and breathing disorders such as asthma or obesity hypoventilation syndrome (OHS).

There are so many negative outcomes of living an unhealthy lifestyle that it's crazy to think that, according to the latest National Health and Nutrition Examination Survey done by the United States, over 2 in 3

Americans are overweight or obese. To get more specific, 64 percent of women and 74 percent of men are overweight or obese.

No wonder everyone thinks these diseases are coming for them — it's the norm to be carrying around all this extra fat.

If you're feeling a little down, get ready to lighten up. Here are the outcomes of living a healthful lifestyle.

Benefits

Now that we've taken a little ride through the pits of despair, let's turn our attention to the land of the healthy. Let's take a look at the positive effects of a healthy lifestyle and see what it has to offer.

Better mood

If you've ever eaten pretty badly for a long period of time (family vacation?) you know what it can do to your mood. A 2014 study in the British Journal of Health Psychology found a link between a healthier diet and an increased sense of engagement and purpose. People who ate more fruits and vegetables were more curious and creative during their day-to-day lives. In other words, your thoughts will simply become more positive, because you're treating your body well.

Think of it this way: if you are eating a healthy diet and exercising consistently, your body will look better. If your body looks better, you'll feel better about your appearance. If you feel better about your appearance, your self-esteem and confidence will improve. If your self-esteem and confidence are riding high, you'll be in a good mood.

There are also certain foods that have been shown to make your body and mind function more effectively. For example, foods like fish, dairy, and grains have been found to moderate the amount of cortisol, the stress hormone, in the body.

Long story short: Eat well, look good, feel good.

Disease prevention

Cardiovascular disease afflicts or kills as many as one in two people in the United States and other developed countries around the world. That means you know a lot of people who have been or will be affected by heart attacks, strokes, and/or other similar conditions.

Here's the good news: you don't have to be one of them. To paraphrase Smokey the Bear, only you can prevent cardiovascular problems!

The best way to do so is to bring a healthy lifestyle pattern into your life. As the Harvard T.H. Chan School of Public Health's Nutrition Source defines it, a healthy lifestyle pattern involves four things:

- Not smoking
- Maintaining a healthy weight
- Exercising
- Choosing a healthy diet

This has been borne out in both men and women. The Nurses' Health Study followed one group of women for 14 years and found that women who followed a healthy lifestyle pattern were 80 percent less likely to develop coronary artery disease. A companion study found similar benefits in men.

Adult onset/type II diabetes is another common but highly preventable disease. Keeping your weight in check and being physically active can help prevent most cases.

Increased productivity

Have you ever been in a "food coma"? Maybe you've experienced the exhausting sensation of eating so much food that you never felt like moving again. Maybe you've simply noticed that you get hit with a wave of sleepiness after you eat.

Well, science is here to help. There are actually some foods — including whole grains, lean meats, low-fat dairy products, and fruits and vegetables — that help your body maintain a consistent energy level. When combined with regular physical activity and exercise, these foods will help your body function like a well-oiled machine. Naturally, this means your productivity will be greatly increased.

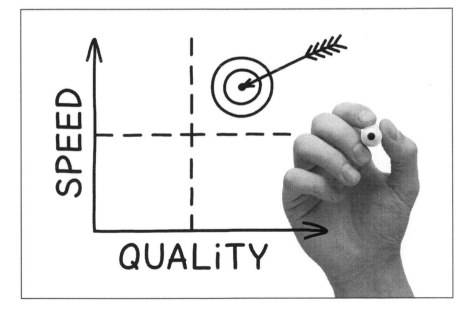

A 2012 study by Population Health Management found that eating an unhealthy diet puts you at a 66 percent increased risk of productivity loss. Another study from 2004 in the Journal of Occupational and Environmental Medicine found an unhealthy diet to be the most dangerous risk factor for low productivity.

Eating healthy won't just help you avoid the "food coma." It will help make your entire life more productive and successful. Sign me up, right?

Increased life span

Here's a simple and instinctive benefit of living a healthy lifestyle: the better you eat, the longer you live.

Think of it this way. Your body is like a car. Its life span is limited, but how long it lasts is largely up to you. If you keep it clean, change the oil, rotate the tires, and maintain it to the best of your abilities, it will last longer. Healthy lifestyle choices have the same effect on your body.

One 2012 study in the Journal of the American Geriatrics Society found that women in their 70s saw an increased life expectancy when eating a diet of fruit and vegetables coupled with regular exercise. Other studies have shown that walking 30 minutes a day increases your life span as well.

It's like any good relationship, really. Be good to your body, and it will stick around longer.

Better sleep

If my experience was any indication, eating and sleeping are two favorite pastimes of college students. The exciting thing is that eating and sleeping actually have a close relationship when it comes to the human body. Eating better can lead to sleeping better, and sleeping better can lead to eating better.

The National Sleep Foundation says that in order to ensure better health, well-being, and general life satisfaction, sleep should be a priority. With the right amount of sleep, you can face the world every day as your most productive self.

It's simple, really. If you're tired and are thinking of sleep all day (or falling asleep all day), it's going to be harder to get things done well and on time. It will also be harder to commit to a healthy diet or exercise if you're just exhausted all the time. It's all connected.

Even something as simple as eating two kiwis before bed can improve your sleep. A 2011 study in Taiwan found that when men and women who struggled with sleep deprivation ate two kiwis one hour before bed for a four-week period, they fell asleep 35 percent faster, slept more soundly, and slept for 13 percent longer. Who doesn't want that?

Higher appeal

If all of that isn't enough, let's throw the cherry on top (wrong topic for this book, but you get the idea). Eating healthy and living a healthy lifestyle have been shown to make you more attractive.

What? That's right. There have been scientific studies showing that a jury of peers sees those who eat more produce as more attractive, with the effect even outweighing a good suntan.

Okay, we're convinced. So, how do we get started?

In the next chapter, we're going to look at what exactly healthy is.

CASE STUDY: RYAN D. ANDREWS, MS, MA, RD, CSCS, NSCA-CPT, ACSM-HFS, CISS

Director of Education — Precision Nutrition
www.precisionnutrition.com

In his career, Ryan Andrews has noted that students should keep nutrition simple and take small steps each day to stay fit and healthy. Andrews advises students to challenge their muscles and mix some sleep into their routines. He feels that eating healthy does not require marathon kitchen sessions; instead, microwave some frozen vegetables, heat some beans, and snack on fresh fruit. Andrews' top advice to students is:

1. Eat real food (e.g., veggies, fruits, beans/legumes, whole grains, nuts/seeds, tea, and water).

2. Do not ever go on a diet.

3. Do something physically active for at least four hours each week.

Ryan D. Andrews, former dietitian at the Johns Hopkins Weight Management Center, is trained in Exercise Physiology (BS, MA, CSCS), Nutrition (MS), and Dietetics (RD, LD). After leaving Johns Hopkins, Andrews began working with Dr. John Berardi as the Director of Education for Precision Nutrition, Inc.

CHAPTER 2

-○-○-○-

What *Is* Healthy?

Have you ever met anyone that just doesn't get sick? They're exposed to sick people all the time, they can drink out of a sick person's water bottle, they can eat a piece of food off the floor, and they just never get sick?

That's a healthy immune system working its magic. According to Karen Frazier, author of "Nutrition Facts: The Truth about Food," being healthy isn't just about not having a disease; it's about your body's ability to keep them away. She explains by quoting the World Health Organization: "Health is a state of complete physical, mental, and social well-being and not merely the absence of disease or infirmity."

So, here we are on the quest for the definition of healthy. In this chapter, we're going to take a look at just about every kind of "healthy" there is. We'll look at the difference between food that's manufactured in a lab (think cereal), and food that's manufactured in the ground (think vegetables). Is there really a difference between organic and regular food or grain-fed vs. grass-fed beef? We're going to look at the difference, and we'll find out if it's really worth splurging on.

What the heck is the difference between whole grain, multigrain, and whole wheat? Are these any better than the old-time favorite, white (think white bread)? What's the low-down on sugar, what's the difference between macro and micronutrients, and is the governmental "food pyramid" really worth following?

This is a pretty hefty chapter. Let's get started.

Power Feeds You

Before we get into all the arguments and debates that make up the next few chapters of this book, it's important to realize that there is a system surrounding our health. Companies exist to make money — not necessarily to ensure that you are healthy. While there are a lot of companies out there that value you and your health, it's safe to say that the majority of corporations do not.

In their book "Whole: Rethinking the Science of Nutrition," T. Colin Campbell and Howard Jacobson explain: "[…] Health information is controlled, and has been for a long time, by interests that are not in alignment with the common good — industries that care much more about their profit than our health" (2013).

Campbell and Jacobson are specifically referring to the pharmaceutical, medical, and food industries. When you actually look into the food industry, you start to see the corruption. Why are there so many processed foods with all these additives and preservatives? It's so that people get addicted to the taste, and also so that stores can keep the food on the shelves longer, which maximizes their profits.

You'll also see "research" that is done explaining the benefits of a certain product, but Campbell and Jacobson say that that can't always be trusted, either. They use the milk industry to explain this one:

> "Dairy interests contribute generous sums of money to many health-related nonprofits as well, thereby influencing their highly effective public pronouncements about the benefits of dairy. These nonprofits have to scramble for funding, so there's pressure not to upset large repeat donors.

> They also pay for academic activity that passes for 'research,' producing studies that start by assuming milk's benefits and then find increasingly creative and dishonest ways to 'prove' those benefits. The mainstream media, to the extent that they are funded by 'Got Milk?' and other dairy industry ads, conveniently ignores, underreports, and casts doubt upon the myriad of studies that show that milk and other dairy products emphatically don't 'do a body good.'

> As newspapers and TV news struggle to stay afloat in the age of digital media, they also are susceptible to the dairy industry's subtle pressure to favor its side of the story."

You can see how corrupt everything is. We now live in a world where you have to question everything you see — who funded the study, what kinds of claims are they making, and why should you trust them?

You always have to keep these things in mind when you hear some huge claim in the news. Most of the time, that huge claim has the power to cause you click on the story, which is why those claims will never die down. They intrigue you, and they end up feeding you.

Always remember that the food industry is an industry after all, and its power is what's stocking your pantry.

Processed vs. Natural Food

The main difference between processed and natural food is the stuff added in. Processed food is usually found in some kind of packaging, which means it needs to be preserved so that it doesn't go bad. You rarely see processed food in a fridge.

Processed food has an ingredient list full of words you may not recognize or understand. There are lots of added sugars in there hiding behind scientific terms.

There are artificial colors added to your food to make it more pleasing to look at, which convinces you to buy it. There are also artificial flavors added, which means that "banana" muffin mix that's sitting on the shelf isn't made with actual bananas. Let's take an in-depth look at artificial colors and flavorings.

Artificial colors

Food dyes are what make that packaged food look so enticing. The colors draw you in, and they make your mouth water. However, the problems that these dyes (such as Red 40 and Yellow 5) cause have led other countries (such as the European Union and the British government) to ban them.

According to the Center for Science in the Public Interest, artificial colors in our food can cause the following reactions:

- Hyperactivity in children
- Behavioral problems
- Allergic reactions
- Cancer

The fact that these chemicals, which only serve the purpose of making food look good, have such horrible effects on our bodies is astounding. More importantly, natural ingredients can replace these chemicals.

Since food dyes are outlawed in Britian, Kellogg's Nutri-Grain bars are made with natural colorings, which include beetroot, Annatto, and Paprika extra to get that red color in the filling. However, in the U.S., food dyes are FDA-approved, so our Nutri-Grain bars contain Red 40, Yellow 6, and Blue 1.

So, why is the FDA not banning food dye? Well, the main reason is because they're blaming the individual for being sensitive. Some people are allergic to food dyes, while others aren't. While researchers still can't pinpoint the exact reason why, there's convincing research that indicates it's in our genes. It's similar to why some people experience a bad reaction to a certain drug, while others don't.

The FDA	Center for Science in the Public Interest
"Children experience a 'unique intolerance' to food dyes."	"Food dyes can be toxic to children's developing bodies."
"We need to do additional testing to prove your claims."	"You haven't required or commissioned any new tests since 2011."
"There is an accepted daily intake (ADI) to ensure safety."	"Dyes have provoked behavioral symptoms far below that ADI."
"We've done tests to come up with the ADI safety system."	"Those tests have not measured any neurobehavioral outcomes."

> **Long story short:** Food dyes can cause negative damages and reactions, and the FDA hasn't done proper testing to back-up these findings. Some individuals are more sensitive to food dyes than others. That's why it isn't banned in the U.S.

Artificial flavors

If you're wondering how a flavor can be artificial, it's a very intricate, chemical process. Here's how it works.

When we eat something, it isn't just our taste buds that are making it taste a certain way. Our sense of smell plays a huge role. We only have four taste sensations: sweet, salty, sour, and bitter. Our nose, on the other hand, can interpret thousands of different smells.

What this means is that anything we eat has an extremely long and complex set of chemicals that work together to produce the final experience. However, there are a few foods, particularly fruits, that have some chemical sets that stick out as more dominant — these chemical sets are what carry most of the flavor to us. According to HowStuffWorks, these dominant chemical sets are called *esters*.

If you can vaguely remember some stuff from biology or chemistry, this chemical component might make some sense to you: the ester called Octyl Acetate, which is $CH_3COOC_5H_{11}$, is the dominant chemical component in orange flavoring.

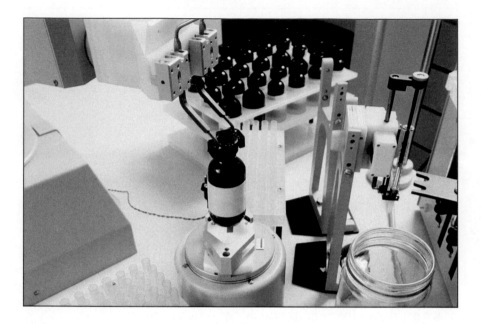

So, once chemists can figure out which chemical sets are the dominant ones, they can manufacture that in a lab by mimicking the chemical components of the real thing. Then, they just inject that ester in your food, and violà, you have orange-flavored gum or banana-flavored muffins.

Now, artificial flavorings are safe to consume, and they don't differ that much from natural flavoring, because the chemical compounds are mimicked. However, here's the problem with them.

This is the part where everything circles back around to money. Since artificial flavorings are made in a lab, scientists can tinker with it in order to maximize the amount of money they'll make. Here's how they do it:

- The taste can be increased so that the flavor is more potent than natural foods. In other words, you begin to crave the bold "strawberry" flavor, because it tastes stronger than the real strawberries you find in the fridge.

- They can make the taste go away faster, causing you to purchase more of it. In a 2011 interview with Morley Safer of *60 Minutes*, two flavor scientists explained that their main goal in life is to make food addictive by causing a burst of intense flavor when you first bite down, and a finish that doesn't linger so that you buy more.

- They make an old product taste new. According to the Environmental Working Group (EWG), when orange juice is pasteurized, some of the orange flavorings start to go away. In order to make you think you're drinking fresh orange juice, flavor scientists insert some of those orange esters into the juice. This makes you think you're drinking fresh orange juice, when in reality, it might be kind of old.

These startling facts about artificially flavored foods have hit the media by storm, being published on platforms like Mashable as well as in hit books, such as "The Dorito Effect" by Mark Schatzker. The simple fact is this: people are starting to get used to the amped up flavorings in processed foods, so when they start to taste the real foods (the ones that come from nature) their taste buds think they're dull.

Do you remember at the beginning of the book where I made this huge claim that it's possible to change your taste buds? That's exactly what Mark Schatzker did. He spent about a year buying only the best, freshest ingredients that he could. He stayed away from artificial ingredients altogether, and he says that his palate has changed drastically. For example, he no longer puts sugar in his coffee, because he feels like the sweetness gets in the way (sound familiar?).

He explains, "Americans now use 600 million pounds of flavorings every year. We have made bland, high calorie food taste thrillingly delicious. And we can't stop eating it. And to make matters worse, whole foods, like tomatoes, chickens and cucumbers, are getting blander and blander. In short, everything that's gone wrong with food and our eating habits can be understood through flavor."

Long story short: While artificial flavors might not necessarily be bad for you, they're being used to make you prefer them over natural food, to addict you to processed food, and to trick you into thinking old products are new.

The next time you get that long lasting craving for those barbecue potato chips, consider where that irresistible craving is coming from.

Organic vs. Conventional Groceries

If you're stuck between organic and regular groceries, you're not alone. Many people don't understand the difference between the two, or they're brainwashed by one side or the other. Let's take an in-depth look at the difference.

According to the European Food Information Council and the U.S. Department of Agriculture, the only difference between organic food and conventional food is the way it's produced and processed.

Organic	Conventional
Fertilizers and pesticides are restricted; no man-made fertilizers, pesticides, growth regulators, and livestock feed additives are allowed	Can use most pesticides, except for a list of pesticides banned by the U.S. Government
Heavily reliant on crop rotation, animal and plant manures, hand-weeding, and biological pest control	Heavily reliant on pesticides, chemical fertilizers, GMO, and heavy irrigation
Severely restrict, and in some cases, ban the use of food additives	Food additives are allowed
Environmentally better — organic farming reduces pollution and conserves water and soil quality	Can be harmful to the environment by creating pollution in the air, water, and soil through the use of chemicals

So, what's the nutrient difference? According to Mayo Clinic, a recent study that examined the past 50 years of scientific articles about this topic found that there is **no significant difference in the nutrient content** between organic and conventional foods.

However, there are still some things to consider. Pesticides are used to produce conventionally grown produce. Pesticides are used to kill living things. The use of pesticides and its link to negative health effects on humans is greatly debated.

Conventional foods are allowed to contain additives, which means they can have preservatives, artificial sweeteners, colorings, flavorings, and monosodium glutamate.

Finally, conventional foods do cause stress on the environment through pollution to air, water, and soil.

There is also the cost difference between traditional produce and organic produce. Synthetic pesticides are cheaper to use than the organic methods, and organic produce don't use waxes or preservatives, so they do spoil faster. Organic produce doesn't look as pretty as conventional produce; you may see odd shapes, varying sizes, and different colors when it comes to organic produce. The lack of chemicals on the produce causes these natural differences.

Here is a chart explaining the pros and cons of organic produce:

Organic pros	Organic cons
Environmentally friendly; uses less energy	More expensive
No added "stuff" like preservatives or flavorings	Spoils faster
No pesticides	Imperfect products
May contain a higher nutritional value	More likely to contain bugs

And here are the pros and cons for conventionally farmed produce:

Conventional pros	Conventional cons
Low cost	May cause health concerns
Lots of job opportunities	May harm the environment
Very profitable	Pushes out small-scale farmers

So, we're trying to get to the truth here. I'd like to cite some studies, but the two most popular studies are (believe it or not) agenda-driven. For the fun of it, here are those studies.

Stanford University	Newcastle University
Has received funding from agriculture business interests in the **conventional** farming sector	Has received funding from agriculture business interests in the **organic** farming sector
Found little to no difference between organic and conventional foods	Found that conventional crops contain 18-69 percent less antioxidants; are four times more likely to contain pesticides; have 48 percent higher concentrations of heavy metals

So, with a completely ambiguous cloud over who to believe, you have to make a decision for yourself.

Different sources suggest different things, but most emphasize the important of mixing and matching. The EWG came up with some key phrases to help us shop better when it comes to organic vs. conventional produce. These are called the Dirty Dozen™ and the Clean Fifteen™. These refer to the twelve types of produce that are the most likely to contain pesticides and the fifteen types of produce that are the least likely.

The Dirty Dozen, as of 2015, contains the following types of produce:

- Apples
- Peaches
- Nectarines
- Strawberries
- Grapes
- Celery
- Spinach
- Sweet bell peppers
- Cucumbers
- Cherry tomatoes
- Imported snap peas
- Potatoes

The EWG found that 99 percent of apples, 98 percent of peaches, and 97 percent of nectarines tested positive for pesticide residue. They also found that a single grape contained 15 pesticides. The results are unsettling for these particular products — if you do decide that you want to buy some organic produce but can't afford it, it's best to splurge on these items (if you can).

The Clean Fifteen contains:

- Avocados
- Sweet corn
- Pineapples
- Cabbage
- Frozen sweet peas
- Onions
- Asparagus
- Mangoes
- Papayas
- Kiwis
- Eggplant
- Grapefruit
- Cantaloupe
- Cauliflower
- Sweet potatoes

These are items that are the least likely to contain pesticide residues. For example, out of all the avocados that were tested, only one percent contained pesticide residues. Only 5.5 percent of these items had multiple pesticide residues. In general, these items are the ones you can more safely buy conventionally.

> **Long story short:** There are pros and cons for both organic and conventionally grown produce. If you don't want to commit to one side, the best thing to do is to mix and match following the Dirty Dozen and the Clean Fifteen guidelines.

Conventionally Fed vs. Grass-Fed Beef

This seems like the great debate of our century — which is better: grass-fed or conventionally fed beef? Proponents of traditional techniques say that grain-fed makes more sense, while advocates of organic food production say that grass-fed beef is a no-brainer.

Let's take a look at what both sides have to say.

Here are three sources that have published articles in favor of grain or corn-fed beef: Beef Magazine, Advocates for Agriculture, and Cooking Light. The specific studies they cite are from Texas A&M University's Department of Animal Science, Texas AgriLife Research Study, and the National Cattlemen's Beef Association.

Here's what they say:

- **Texas A&M University's Department of Animal Science:** They studied the difference between ground beef from grass-fed cattle and traditional, grain-fed cattle on risk factors for cardiovascular disease (CVD) and type II diabetes in men. They found that the grass-fed beef was not more healthful. Grass-fed beef is higher in saturated and trans fat (2014).

- **Texas AgriLife Research Study:** Researchers found that grass-fed beef has no beneficial effects on plasma lipid. The article from Advocates for Agriculture says, "High monounsaturated fat ground beef from grain-fed cattle increased HDL cholesterol, increased LDL particle diameters, and decreased insulin, suggesting that ground beef produced by intensive production practices provides 'a healthful, high-quality source of protein'" (2010).

- **National Cattlemen's Beef Association:** A spokeswoman for the association says that if you feed cows grass instead of grain or corn, you do increase the omega-3 content, but "if you look at it in terms of a whole diet, it's not a significant advantage to human health" (no date is mentioned).

I must say that in trying to find advocates of grain-fed or corn-fed cattle, I did have a slightly more difficult time. There are far more resources (on the Web) that are supporters of grass-fed cattle. So, while I am citing three sources on each side of the argument, be aware that there are many more voices speaking up on the grass-fed side of the debate (for what it's worth).

So, as promised, here are three advocates for grass-fed beef: Grassfed Network, The Grassfed Exchange, and Eat Wild.

- **Grassfed Network:** The benefits of grass-fed beef include higher levels of vitamin A, D, and K. Also, they don't have the hormones and antibiotics that traditionally raised cattle do. There is something called Conjugated Linoleic Acid (CLA), which is in the fat of grass-fed animals. This is known to fight cancer, manage weight, and build muscle. Also, folic acid is 50 to 100 times higher in grass-fed animals. As far as eggs go, you can see the difference in the yolk color: grass-fed eggs are a very dark orange (nutrient-dense) while traditional eggs are a much lighter yellow (2012).

- **The Grassfed Exchange:** Grass-fed beef is leaner in total lipids, higher in CLA, higher in omega-3s, and higher in vitamins A and E (2016).

- **Eat Wild:** Grass-fed beef lowers your "bad" LCL cholesterol levels. Grass-fed meat is also lower in calories and higher in omega-3s, which reduces our risk of cancer, reduces the risk of high blood pressure, and reduces the risk of having a heart attack by 50 percent. Omega-3s are also great for your brain, making it less likely that you'll suffer from a brain-related disease like depression or Alzheimer's. Grass-fed beef is also higher in CLAs, which "may be one of our most potent defenses against cancer" (no specific date is mentioned).

Now, to make everything much easier to read, let's put everything we know into two lists of pros and cons.

Pros of grass-fed beef	Cons of grass-fed beef
Higher vitamin, CLA, folic acid, and omega-3 levels	Harder to find
Lower bad LCL cholesterol levels	Expensive
No hormones or antibiotics used	Can be more difficult to cook properly
Reduced risk of cancer and other diseases	
Fewer calories	

Pros of grass-fed beef	Cons of grass-fed beef
Much cleaner (multinational food corporations are known for having sanitary issues)	
Better taste (more tender, leaner, and juicier than grain-fed beef)	
Better environment for the animals	

The most resounding pro among all grass-fed beef lovers is the taste. Almost every source I could find had something to say about the immense improvement in flavor.

Pros of conventionally-fed beef	Cons of conventionally-fed beef
Cheaper	Less sanitary
Easier to find	Fewer health benefits
Convenient for the farmer (much quicker)	Poorer taste
Many researchers say that there are no health benefits to eating grass-fed beef; some even say that grain-fed is better for you	Higher levels of bad fats
	More animal cruelty

Overall, the biggest complaint about grass-fed beef is how expensive it is. So, while it seems that grass-fed beef is better in so many ways, if you don't have room for it in your budget, you're stuck in a tough spot.

Whole Grain vs. Multigrain vs. Whole Wheat

All of these terms can be confusing. They all look the same, but are they actually different?

The free USDA Cookbook for Schools (found at **www.whatscooking. fns.usda.gov**) says that you should aim to make at least half of your grains whole grains: "Look for the words '100% whole grain' or '100% whole wheat' on the food label. Whole grains provide more nutrients, like fiber, than refined grains."

Okay, so we know we're supposed to go for the "whole" stuff, but what's the difference between whole grain, multigrain, and whole wheat? Here's the low-down.

- **Multigrain** means that more than one grain is used to make the product. For example, the product you're holding might have some whole wheat flour as well as some barley flour.

- **Whole grain** means that the entire grain is used in the product, which means it includes the bran, the germ, and the endosperm.

- **Whole wheat** is actually a kind of whole grain. The Oldways Whole Grain Council explains: "We all know that all carrots are vegetables but not all vegetables are carrots. It's similar with whole wheat and whole grain: Whole wheat is one kind of whole grain, so all whole wheat is whole grain, but not all whole grain is whole wheat."

Now that we know the difference, which one is the healthiest?

Registered dietitian Carrie Dennett explains that multigrain products contain more than one grain, but that doesn't make it better for you (2014): "they may be refined and stripped of their natural nutrients and fiber."

Whole grain, on the other hand, contains all parts of the grain, so you know you're getting all the benefits that come along with eating grains.

Long story short: To make sure you're always getting the most nutritious products, look at the ingredient label. Make sure that the top ingredient says "whole" in front of it. If it doesn't, you're not reaping the nutrient and fiber benefits of whole grain products.

Sugar

Throughout history, people have tried to blame a single ingredient in food for the massive failure of the SAD. (Standard American Diet, if you forgot.)

Schatzker explains this evolution of thought (2015): "A year or two ago, a panic over high-fructose corn syrup came through like a flash flood and then died down to a trickle. Saturated fat, which used to be deadly, is enjoying a renaissance while polyunsaturated fat, which at one time was seen as the antidote to saturated fat, is now under attack. Before fat it was carbs and before carbs it was fat, and if you go back far enough sugar pops up again."

In other words, here's the evolution of the blame game:

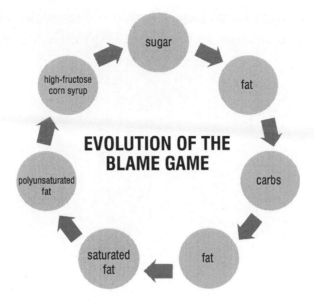

No matter what the order of the blame game is, we see this trend of trying to blame a single... well, a single *thing* for the failure of the SAD.

While blaming a single thing for the huge problem would be convenient, Schatzker explains that that just isn't going to work. "Food is complicated," he says.

That's why this book isn't just about banning one thing from your diet — it's about figuring out what works for you. However, sugar is an actual problem, and while deleting it from your diet might not fix everything, it can definitely help.

Here's why: sugar is full of calories and is completely void of nutrients. In other words, you're consuming empty calories. You're getting quick energy, and that's about it. Added sugar does nothing good for you. In fact, it does a lot of bad things to you.

Sugar feeds bacteria in your mouth, causing tooth decay. Too much fructose can damage your liver. (Fructose is mainly found in added sugars). Sugar causes the insulin in your body to become resistant, causing diseases like type II diabetes. Having constantly elevated insulin levels (caused by eating a ton of sugar) contributes to cancer.

Multiple studies show the correlation between sugar consumption and cancer: Stephen Seely and David Horrobin's research published in *Medical Hypotheses* (1983), Roberd Bostick and seven other researchers who published their findings in *Cancer Causes & Control Cancer Causes Control* (1994), M. L. Slattery and six other researchers who published in *Food and Chemical Toxicology* (1997), and Lorraine Lipscombe's research published in *Insulin Resistance and Cancer* (2011).

Another huge problem with sugar is that it doesn't make us feel full. We can eat something full of sugar, and within 30 minutes, we're hungry again. Researchers decided to do a study on this concept, and they found out that this is absolutely the case. Kathleen Page and 10 other researchers published a study in *Jama* (2013) where they tested hunger levels. They gave one group a fructose-filled drink (an added sugar), and they gave the other group a glucose-filled drink (a natural sugar that our bodies naturally produce).

The fructose-drinking group had much less activity in the satiety center of the brain, and they were also hungrier than the glucose group. The hunger hormone in the brain was significantly lowered for the glucose group in comparison to the fructose group.

> **Long story short:** Sugar doesn't make us feel full, and it doesn't provide any kind of nutritional benefit. Added sugars are truly useless.

Understanding Macro and Micronutrients

Let's start this off with an easy-to-understand chart, courtesy Unicef.

Macronutrients	Micronutrients
Proteins	Vitamins
Carbohydrates	Minerals
Fat	Trace elements

Macronutrients are required in large amounts to give you energy. Proteins contain substances like enzymes, hormones, and antibodies. Carbohydrates include sugars, starches, celluloses, and gums. Fats contain glycerol and fatty acids. You need all three to live.

Micronutrients are needed to help your body function. They set off chemical reactions in your body. There are a lot of micronutrients, so here is a complete list of them with small explanations that let you know what it does for you.

Vitamins

- **Vitamin A:** This vitamin is needed for healthy vision, bone development, and healthy mucous membranes. It is found in deep yellow and orange fruits as well as vegetables, liver, fish liver oils, dairy products, and egg yolks.

- **Vitamin D:** This vitamin is needed for healthy bones, and it increases the absorption of calcium and other minerals. It is found in sunshine and fish liver oils, and is frequently added to milk.

- **Vitamin E:** This vitamin works with other nutrients to keep your blood cells and other body components running smoothly. It is found in vegetable oils, nuts, green leafy vegetables, and wheat germ.

- **Vitamin K:** This vitamin helps your blood to clot properly. It can be found in green, leafy vegetables and alfalfa.

Vitamins A, D, E, and K are all fat-soluble, meaning they need to be eaten with a little fat in order for your body to absorb them properly. It also means your body stores them in fat, and it's possible to get too much A, D, and K. If you take a supplement of these vitamins, be careful not to take more than 100 percent of the U.S. Recommended Daily Allowance (RDA).

- **Vitamin B1 (thiamine):** Scientists used to believe there was just one B vitamin, but over time, they discovered that it was actually many different nutrients. Thus, we have the various B vitamins you see listed. This vitamin is needed for metabolizing carbohydrates, and things can get pretty grim without it (depression, cardiac failure, and kidney problems, to name a few). It can be found in meats, including organ meats, fish, and poultry, and in nuts and whole grains. Enriched cereals and flour frequently contain thiamine and some of the other B vitamins.

- **Vitamin B2 (riboflavin):** This vitamin helps to keep your lips, eyes, and mouth healthy. It can be found in organ meats, milk, eggs, and green, leafy vegetables.

- **Vitamin B3 (niacin):** This vitamin helps to rid the body of harmful chemicals, it improves circulation, and it lowers your cholesterol level. It can be found in meat, poultry, fish, nuts, and whole grains.

- **Vitamin B5 (pantothenic acid):** This vitamin helps to metabolize carbohydrates, protein, and fats. It is found in whole grains, nuts, meats, and eggs. The word *pantothenic* comes from a Greek word meaning "from everywhere," because this vitamin is easy to find.

- **Vitamin B6 (pyroxidine):** This vitamin is important for your nervous system and complex body functions. It can be found in meat, poultry, fish, and vegetables, including potatoes.

- **Vitamin B7 (biotin):** This vitamin helps to metabolize fat and protein and is necessary for the growth of your cells. Fortunately, bacteria in your intestines produce more than enough of this vitamin, but just in case, it is also in tomatoes, romaine lettuce, and carrots, among other foods.

- **Vitamin B9 (folic acid):** This vitamin helps to mature your red blood cells and keep your nervous system healthy. It is found in liver, eggs, poultry, fish, and green leafy vegetables.

- **Vitamin B12 (actually a group called cobalamins):** This vitamin group helps with forming your blood and works with your nervous system, including your brain. Some people do not process it properly and have a condition known as pernicious anemia. It is found in liver, shellfish, and milk.

- **Choline (one of the B vitamins; without its own number):** This vitamin helps the liver to function properly. It is found in egg yolk, soy, and liver.

- **Vitamin C:** This vitamin helps your immune system and also helps with iron absorption. Without it, your wounds would heal poorly and you would bleed too easily. It is found in many foods, including citrus fruits, strawberries, melon, tomato, and broccoli.

The B vitamins and vitamin C are water-soluble. This means you are not as likely to overdose on them because if you consume too much, you will generally pass the excess on your bathroom break. If you are wondering what happened to the other B vitamins, they turned out not to be vitamins after all and were disqualified.

There are also higher B numbers, which have not yet been proven to be vitamins.

Vitamin A	0 %	
Vitamin C	2 %	
Calcium	45 %	
Iron	0 %	
Vitamin D	60 %	
Thiamine	15 %	
Niacin	15 %	
Vitamin B6	15 %	
Folate	8 %	
Pantothenate	15 %	
Phosphorus	20 %	
Magnesium		
Zinc		
Manganese		

Minerals

Minerals are inorganic substances from the earth, in contrast to vitamins, which are of plant, animal, or bacterial origin. You need an adequate intake of the following minerals:

- **Calcium:** Your body needs calcium to build strong bones and teeth. It is also necessary for your cells, muscles, nerves, and heart. A deficiency can cause numerous problems, such as osteoporosis. Good sources are milk products, oysters, salmon, and sardines.

- **Chloride:** Chloride is involved in the body's metabolism and in keeping a proper acid-base balance in the blood. Almost all Americans get plenty of chloride in table salt.

- **Copper:** Copper helps your bones, immune system, and circulatory system. Most Americans are never deficient in copper, because it leaks into our water system through copper piping. It can be found in beef, nuts, liver, mackerel, beans, and lentils.

- **Iodine:** This mineral helps our body regulate our metabolism. In the past, many Americans were deficient in iodine, but it is now added to most table salt. It is also found in seafood.

- **Iron:** Iron is necessary to keep our blood healthy. A deficiency can lead to anemia. It is found in organ meats, including liver, and in egg yolks, meat, poultry, and dark green vegetables.

- **Magnesium:** This mineral is necessary for healthy bones, teeth, muscles, and nerves. It is also involved in metabolism. It can be found in milk products, meat, nuts, and legumes.

- **Manganese:** Manganese helps us with enzyme processes, metabolism, wound healing, and bone development. Good sources of manganese include tofu, nuts, seeds, oysters, whole grains, and chocolate.

- **Molybdenum:** This mineral is an enzymatic component that helps our bodies turn food into energy. There has never been a known deficiency in this mineral. Beans, lentils, nuts, and milk products are good sources.

- **Nickel:** Nickel assists the functioning and distribution of other nutrients, including iron, in our bodies. It can be found in lentils, oatmeal, nuts, and cocoa.

- **Phosphorus:** This mineral plays several important roles in our bodies, including helping in the development of bones and teeth. A deficiency can lead to stunted growth. It can be found in milk products, eggs, meat, poultry, fish, and nuts.

- **Potassium:** Potassium is critical in nerve and muscle health, among other functions. A serious deficiency can lead to a heart arrhythmia. It can be found in most fruits and vegetables, especially citrus, melons, and bananas.

- **Selenium:** This mineral is involved in metabolism and thyroid functions. Good sources of selenium include butter, garlic, whole grains, nuts, seeds, fish, and liver.

- **Sodium:** Sodium is essential for fluid balance and healthy nerves and muscles. Americans consume plenty of sodium in table salt.

- **Sulfur:** This mineral helps to create our hair, skin, and nails. It is found in meat, milk products, eggs, fish, and nuts.

- **Zinc:** Zinc is important to the immune system, muscle growth, and healthy skin. Good sources include meat, poultry, seafood, whole grains, nuts, and eggs.

Good carbs vs. bad carbs

Carbs are looked at as the devil by many dieters, with some of the most popular diets being that you exclude carbs from your meal plan. We're on the mission to figure out if they're really as bad as many think they are.

According to Elaine Magee, MPH, RD, nationally known as "The Recipe Doctor," the main difference between good carbs and bad carbs is the fiber content. Fiber does a lot of good things for your body, including helping with healthy bowel movements, lowering your cholesterol, and controlling your blood sugar levels. Fiber also makes you feel more full, which helps you to control how much you eat.

A lot of processed carbs are stripped of their fiber (white bread and white rice). Natural sources of carbohydrates are full of the beneficial stuff (fruits and vegetables).

Another bad way to get carbs is through added sugars. While many people opt for low-fat or fat-free items, they don't realize that fat is being replaced by added sugars in the form of carbs.

The typical SAD is full of fiberless carbs like bagels made with white flour, white hamburger buns, and flour tortillas. If we can switch to carbs that actually do something good for us, we're one step closer to living a healthier life. Those good carbs are fruits, vegetables, beans, and whole grains.

Good fat vs. bad fat

It seems like just about everything has been scrutinized at one point or another for being bad. Fat is no exception.

Perhaps you've noticed while walking down the grocery aisle that nearly every item has some low-fat alternative: low-fat sour cream, skim milk, or low-fat mozzarella cheese. America is obsessed with cutting out the fat — but, why?

We need fat to survive. The USDA recommends that we get about 25-30 percent of our calories from fat, and scientifically, we need at least 10 percent of our calories from fat just to survive. The problem is, when you break fat down, you notice that it's very calorie-dense. That means that a meal that's high in fat will be higher in calories because of the fat content. So, while fat is delicious *and* nutritious, it can cause us to gain weight if we eat too much of it.

Beyond the simple facts comes the confusion of good fats and bad fats. We've all heard about how good olive oil and avocados are for us, but what about French fries and ice cream? Let's dive in.

According to Kathleen M. Zelman, MPH, RD, LD, writer for WebMD (2007), good fats are unsaturated (which include mono- and polyunsaturated fats). These fats lower your cholesterol and reduce your risk for heart disease. The fats that contain omega-3s are the real winners for your health. Think salmon, flaxseed, and walnuts.

Saturated fats fall somewhere in the middle. They aren't great for you, but they aren't as bad as trans fats. Most animal products have saturated fats in them. Think poultry skin, full fat dairy products, and eggs.

On the other hand, the bad fats are trans fats. These fats raise your cholesterol, clog your arteries, and raise your risk for heart disease. This is the fat that makes up your junk food products — fried foods, cookies, icing, and popcorn — basically all the stuff we love, right? This type of fat dramatically raises your bad cholesterol and lowers your good cholesterol.

Don't avoid fat, but choose it wisely.

Protein

Finally, we land at protein. Protein is generally accepted as one of the good things to include in your diet due to its ability to enhance growth and development. Every single cell in your body contains protein, which means your body needs it to function.

Your body can only functionally use about .8 grams of protein for every pound you weigh. For example, a 150-pound person can use up to about 120 grams of protein in their daily diet. If you consume more than that, your body doesn't really know what to do with it, so it stores it as fat. That means that an excessively high protein diet isn't going to do you much good.

However, consuming the right amount of protein for your body is pretty awesome. Protein makes you feel more full. A study published in The American Journal of Clinical Nutrition (2005) found that participants that increased their protein intake from 15 percent up to 30 percent ate

441 fewer calories each day. They weren't even trying; they found that they were more full on less food.

It is important to note that they didn't start eating only protein — they raised their level up to 30 percent. Make sure that you aren't overconsuming.

Not only does protein make you feel more full, but it helps build muscle, it's good for your bones, it can reduce cravings, and it can boost your metabolism. No matter what diet or lifestyle you choose to take on, be sure that you don't neglect or overeat protein.

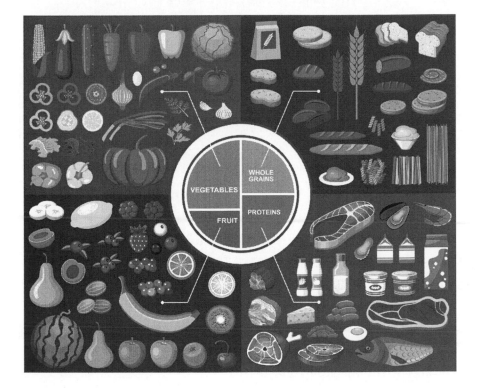

The USDA "MyPlate"

The old USDA food pyramid has been replaced by what is now called "MyPlate." It's a plate-shaped diagram (much easier to understand) that shows you what should be on your plate. Half of your meal should be fruits and vegetables (slightly more vegetables than fruit), a quarter should be grains, and the other quarter should be protein. There's also a small spot for dairy, which is represented by a glass.

It sounds pretty wholesome, but people are still skeptical about it. Writer Peter Smith suggests that the USDA's agenda peaks through: he thinks they're trying to get people to eat less meat.

Dieticians weigh in on the pyramid, providing both pros and cons to the new structure. Most liked the fact that the plate stresses fruits and vegetables, which most Americans don't eat enough of. However, the issues with the plate revolve around things that aren't explained. For example, how big is the plate? What a short female eats compared to a tall male is going to be completely different, and MyPlate doesn't address that.

Another issue is: how often should you be eating this plate of food? What if someone eats around six times a day? Grace Derocha, a registered dietician, explains (2011): "There is no mention of the ideal quantity for each food group nor how often one should eat them."

Also, there's no mention of fat on the plate. After all, the building blocks of nutrition are carbohydrates, fats, and proteins. How can you completely cut one group out?

There is no mention of sweets on the plate, either. It's hard to imagine that even the strictest of eaters isn't going to splurge every once in a while.

Derocha also explains that you should eat differently based on what your goals are: "In the end, I think MyPlate can be a useful nutrition tool, but it has to come with more explanation and education so users can better understand how to apply it properly. People have different physical characteristics and different goals, from weight loss to weight gain and more."

While the intentions of MyPlate are solid — pay attention to what you're putting on your plate — the execution leaves a lot out. It isn't a complete guide to healthful living, and while it may be able to help you visualize what your plate should like look, it doesn't do much beyond that.

CASE STUDY: DEIRDRE WILLIAMS, MS, RD, LDN

8 Melton Road
Brighton, MA 02135
williams_deirdre@yahoo.com

Deirdre Williams says that balance is important for college students: "I think college students need to focus on balance. College can be a time of a tremendous amount of stress from numerous factors: academic demands, poor diet, social pressures, poor sleeping patterns, time constraints, managing parental expectations, financial issues, and many more. Finding a healthy balance by setting priorities and managing time efficiently, keeping expectations realistic, getting adequate sleep, exercising on a regular and consistent basis, eating a healthful and complete diet, seeking support when necessary, and managing finances are essential. This is by no means an easy task."

Her top advice includes:

1. Exercise is essential. Regular physical activity helps to maintain weight in many ways. The more you move, the more calories you use, which keeps weight in check. In addition, regular exercise has been shown to help manage stress, regulate sleep patterns, improve energy levels, sharpen mental acuity, and boost self-confidence.

2. Focus on fluid. Drinking plenty of water is crucial. Aim for at least six to eight glasses per day, and even more if you are highly active or live in a hot climate. Inadequate fluid intake can result in headaches, fatigue, chapped lips, dizziness, and dehydration. Furthermore, limiting sugary drinks, caffeine-laced liquids, and nutrient-poor libations is a healthy habit for all college students. These beverages are full of nutrient-poor "empty" calories, which can lead to weight gain. Caffeine and alcohol also disrupt sleep patterns and can exacerbate stress.

3. Eat regular meals. Try to consume at least four to six small meals or snacks each day. Do not skip meals, as this can diminish energy levels and mental sharpness, decrease metabolism, and lead to overeating later in the day. Late night eating often consists of pizza, fried foods, burritos, and other high-calorie, high-fat foods. Eating small meals at regular intervals during the day can help reduce the urge to eat high-calorie foods late at night.

Deirdre Williams has an MS in nutrition from Boston University. She is a registered and licensed dietitian, currently practicing in Boston, Massachusetts.

CHAPTER 3

❍-❍-❍

Popular Diets Explained

We're all confused. There are all these diets floating around with these huge claims and intense before and after pictures. Which diet should you choose? Should you even choose one of them?

You may decide that you want to jumpstart your healthy life with one of these diets. You may find that you want to use one of them for the rest of your life. You may think that these diets are a complete waste of time, and you'll use other methods of healthy eating instead.

Whatever your final decision is will be completely up to you. However, this all-inclusive chapter will give you the information you need to come to a smart conclusion. The experts even say that no diet is the perfect answer — if there was a single way to go, we'd all be healthy. Matt Fitzgerald, author of "Diet Cults: The Surprising Fallacy at the Core of Nutrition Fads and a Guide to Healthy Eating for the Rest of Us," explains that science hasn't figured it out:

> "In fact, [science] has come as close as possible (because you can't prove a negative) to confirming that there is no such thing as the healthiest diet. To the contrary, science has established quite definitively that humans are able to thrive equally well on a variety of diets."

It seems like every other week an article comes out explaining how horrible a certain diet is, and then the next week, an article comes out telling you how great it is. We're all confused. As we should be.

To get to core of each of these fad diets, each section of this chapter will be split up into four parts:

- What is it?
- Where did it come from?
- What are the pros and cons?
- What is the expected cost?

There's a lot of information to take in, so you might want to pick out the diets that are the most interesting to you and go from there.

The Paleo Diet™

What is it?

The goal of this diet is to mimic how pre-agricultural hunter-gatherers ate. We're basically taking a step back and eating like our ancestors did before all of this factory-made mass-farming stuff started. If the caveman couldn't eat it, then neither can you.

There are seven main components of this diet (**www.thepaleodiet.com**):

1. Higher protein intake
2. Lower carbohydrate intake and lower glycemic index
3. Higher fiber intake
4. Moderate to higher fat intake (mono and polyunsaturated fats with balanced Omega-3 and Omega-6 fats)
5. Higher potassium and lower sodium intake
6. Net dietary alkaline load that balances dietary acid
7. Higher intake of vitamins and minerals

To read more on these seven main components, visit The Paleo Diet website.

Where did it come from?

This diet started with Dr. Loren Cordain, the world's leading expert on the evolutionary basis of diet and disease (**www.thepaleodiet.com**). He published the book "The Paleo Diet," and has come out with several revisions as well as component books, such as cookbooks and guides for athletes.

Cordain was an athlete in college, and he became interested in improving his athletic performance. As he continued his education, he started shaping his ideas about diet and nutrition. Finally, he read "Paleolithic Nutrition" by Dr. Boyd Eaton in about 1987. This concept made perfect sense to him, and he created what we now call The Paleo Diet.

What are the pros and cons?

Is this diet a good fit for you? Well, let's take a look at the pros and cons.

The most important part of a diet is what you're going to be eating. So, here's a list of what you can and cannot eat, which might be a pro or con for you depending on what you like.

Eat	Don't eat
Grass-produced meats	Cereal grains
Fish/seafood	Legumes
Fresh fruits and veggies	Dairy
Eggs	Refined sugar
Nuts and seeds	Potatoes
Healthful oils (olive, walnut, flaxseed, macadamia, avocado, coconut)	Refined vegetable oils
	Salt
	Processed foods

If you can't live without your cheese or your mashed potatoes, this diet might not be for you. If the items listed on the left sound great, you might be a match with this diet.

Beyond the actual food you'd be eating, here's a simplified pros and cons chart.

Pros	Cons
The types of food in this diet are proven to be extremely beneficial to your body	There is no evidence (yet) that excluding dairy, legumes, and grains is beneficial in any way
Studies show that this diet improves several chronic diseases	The evolutionary arguments that are the basis of the diet don't really hold up
This diet highlights how sad our 21st century Western diet really is	Following a "good" and "bad" list of foods is generally problematic for most people
You do not have to count calories	The food today does not resemble the food of yesteryear (for example, meat is fattier today, and most of it is grain-fed, not grass-fed)

What is the expected cost?

The cost of a Paleo diet is going to be higher than the SAD. Well, most of the diets in this chapter (and healthy eating in general) will be more expensive than processed foods.

There are a lot of websites that explain how to eat Paleo on a budget.

One site says that if you switch from a regular diet to a Paleo one, you can expect to spend about $100 more a month (**www.ultimatepaleoguide.com**).

In general, avoid the center of the grocery store. Only shop on the outside part of the store; this is where you will find the fresh ingredients.

Eggs and veggies are relatively cheap, so the only items you'll be splurging on are grass-fed cuts of meat and fruit.

You can also save money by going to your local farmer's market. Another money-saving tip is to grocery shop the day you're going to be cooking. You can often find cuts of meat that are about to expire, which will save you some cash.

Ketogenic

What is it?

Ketogenic eating refers to eating high fat, low carb (HFLC). When you eat this way, your body produces ketones in the liver, which are used for energy. Basically, this diet forces your body to stop using glucose, which comes from carbs, for energy.

When your body doesn't get that glucose for energy, it goes into a state of ketosis. Ketosis is when your body produces ketones for energy, which come from fats breaking down in the liver.

In the end, the goal of eating Ketogenic is to train your body to stop using carbs for fuel and to shift to using fats for fuel. It's recommended to stay around the 15-30g of carbs range per day.

The ideal breakdown of your macronutrients should look like this:

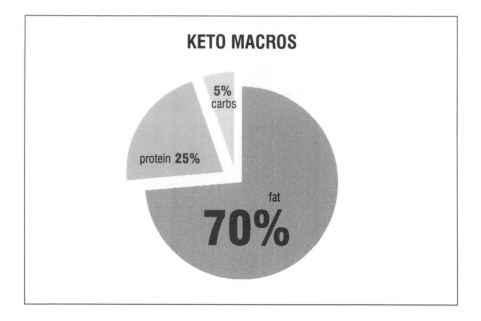

KETO MACROS

5%
carbs

protein 25%

fat

70%

Where did it come from?

According to The Charlie Foundation for Ketogenic Therapies, this diet began in 1924 by Dr. Russell Wilder at the Mayo Clinic. The Ketogenic diet originated as a therapy for epilepsy. It was an alternative to fasting, which was also proven to stop the epilepsy.

What are the pros and cons?

I think the best way to go about this is to first take a look at what you can and cannot eat, similar to what we did for the last section. If there's something you have to have in your diet, this is a good way to find out if the diet just isn't for you.

In general, the focus is obviously on eating fats, which will be your main source for fuel. Some of the fats that are approved for this diet are:

- Avocado
- Beef tallow
- Butter
- Chicken fat
- Ghee
- Non-hydrogenated lard
- Macadamia nuts

- Mayonnaise
- Olive oil
- Coconut oil
- Coconut butter
- Red palm oil
- Peanut butter

There's also an emphasis on buying products that come from grass-fed sources, not grain-fed. So, when you go to buy butter, you'd want to look for a brand that sells organic or grass-fed butter, such as Kerrygold.

Here are the other general food items that are encouraged:

- Fish/Shellfish
- Whole eggs
- Grass-fed meat
- Pork
- Poultry
- Bacon and sausage
- High nutrient/low carb veggies like asparagus, broccoli, and spinach
- Full-fat dairy items like heavy whipping cream and sour cream
- Nuts and seeds
- Water, coffee, and tea
- Sweeteners like stevia, erythritol, and xylitol (preferably the liquid forms)

The items that are off-limits are generally foods with lots of carbs or sugars, since the goal is to feed your body with fat. Here are some things to watch out for on this diet:

- High-carb spices like onion powder and cinnamon
- Fruit
- Tomato based products
- Peppers
- Diet soda
- Medicine
- Chocolate

A definite con of this diet is going to be letting go of high-carb foods. You'll have to ditch the rice, the tortillas, and the baked goods. You'll also have to cut out most fruits from your diet, though many Ketogenic experts say that you can insert small portions of berries.

Here are some other pros and cons to consider:

Pros	Cons
Improved fat loss	It's difficult to stay away from carbohydrates
Improvement for those with epilepsy	Eating out/going to social functions can be a challenge
Fights cancer cells by starving them	When you enter ketosis, your breath and urine have a bad odor
Higher energy levels as well as feeling full more often	Many go too far and cut out fruits and vegetables entirely, causing adverse health effects

What is the expected cost?

The great thing about eating Ketogenic is that the cost is pretty low. In general, fats are not that expensive, and they also last a bit longer because they make you feel full faster. You won't be spending money on processed foods or many fruits, and the meat portion of your diet isn't very high, so you won't have to worry about splurging much there.

In general, a serving of a Ketogenic meal ranges from 50 cents to $2. You can expect to spend about as much as you normally do on groceries.

Weight Watchers

What is it?

This is a weight loss program that is based on either attending weekly meetings or by participating through the online program. This does cost, and the price fluctuates depending on what exactly you sign up for and how long you sign up for it.

Based on a 3-month subscription, here are some figures quoted from the Weight Watchers website:

Online*Plus*	Meetings + Online*Plus*	Coaching + Online*Plus*
$3.84/week	$8.84/week	$10.77/week

When it's all said and done, you'll be spending (initially) between about $50 to $140 to start, depending on which plan you choose.

Online*Plus* is basically an online platform that gives you the tools you need to track and manage your eating habits. There is an app you can use that features recipes, tracking devices, the ability to share your progress, and also the ability to sync up to your fitness devices.

The meetings are in-person, and they are with other people in the program. They help to keep you accountable. These last between 30-45 minutes per session.

The coaching tool is actually a single person that works with you one-on-one. This person helps to keep you motivated. Your coach also comes up with an action plan to meet your needs and keep you on track.

The general idea of Weight Watchers is that different foods are assigned a point value based on fiber and fat content. You are given a certain number of points per day, and the foods you eat must stay under that specified point value.

The main emphasis of the program is staying involved through support systems.

Where did it come from?

This program started in the early 1960s by founder Jean Nidetch. She gathered women into her New York home once a week to talk about losing weight. Two years later, she established the company and held her first public meeting.

In 1978, the company was bought out by H. J. Heinz Company, and now you will see tons of products, from a food line to cookbooks, that are endorsed by the logo.

What are the pros and cons?

The easiest way to go about this is through a simple chart.

Pros	Cons
You can eat whatever you want	While you may be losing weight, you might be causing harm to your health by eating foods that are full of salt and sugar
Weight loss	It's expensive
More likely to learn about nutrition through meetings with experts	Lots of people do not like the group atmosphere of meetings
Slow weight loss is encouraged, which can help you keep it off	Tracking weight loss every week can be discouraging

A lot of people do like the fact that you can eat whatever you want. It discourages the binge-eating that I dare say most of us have experienced, and instead reinforces the importance of small indulgences every once in a while.

There have been many studies done by researchers, and most do show that members are highly likely to lose weight on the program compared to dieting alone.

The accountability factor is often what people need to stay healthy. The biggest problem about this program is that you have to pay for it on top of the groceries you already have to buy. This can turn a lot of people off to the program.

What is the expected cost?

So, on top of buying your weekly groceries, you still have to pay for the program. You can buy whatever food you want, but if you do decide to purchase the food items with the Weight Watchers endorsement, you'll find that they are a tad pricier than their generic counterparts.

You can expect to spend a nice chunk of change on just the program itself, so make sure you still have enough cash for the food.

The Atkins Diet™

What is it?

The Atkins diet is a diet that is based on lowering your carb intake. Similar to Ketogenic eating, the idea is that your body will shift from burning carbohydrates to burning fat for fuel.

You do not count calories on this diet, just carbs. You start out with 20g of carbs a day, and then you gradually increase until you find your perfect carbohydrate level.

You choose the plan you want to follow: Atkins 20™ or Atkins40™ depending on what your goals are.

Where did it come from?

Dr. Atkins, a cardiologist, started advising his patients to lower their sugar and carbohydrate levels, and he found that they were successfully losing weight. He published his first diet book, "Dr. Atkins' Diet Revolution" in 1972, and the Atkins Diet was born. Since then, it has taken off, and millions swear by the diet to keep off the pounds.

You can learn more at **www.atkins.com**.

What are the pros and cons?

The pros and cons of the Atkins Diet are going to be similar to the Ketogenic diet, because the goal is to enter ketosis.

Pros	Cons
Weight loss	Bad breath and tiredness
Cuts out extra sugar; provides you with more energy and less cravings	Constipation
Reduces risk of diabetes and insulin resistance	Possible risk for heart disease because of excess saturated fat

Research clashes for the Atkins Diet; about half say that the excess fat hurts you, and the other half say that this kind of diet is actually an improvement for your heart and cholesterol levels.

What is the expected cost?

According to Super Skinny Me's website, the Atkins diet costs about $100/week, which makes it one of the most expensive diet options out there behind Jenny Craig and NutriSystem.

The diet is based on the book "The New Atkins for a New You: The Ultimate Diet for Shedding Weight and Looking Great," which costs about $16.

Atkins products are also available at grocery stories (such as bars, shakes, and frozen dinners), and those range in price as well.

There are online tools, and those are free. The app as well as all of the online features such as recipes, meal plans, and food lists are free.

You can expect to spend quite a bit of money if you purchase the Atkins food in the grocery store, but the concept can be used to purchase regular groceries, which would be a lot cheaper.

Gluten-Free

What is it?

This one is often a touchy subject for some, because it has caused a lot of controversy and debate within the last few years. The main purpose of eating gluten-free is to treat those with celiac disease or those who are sensitive to gluten.

Scientists and researchers say that for those who don't have celiac disease, a gluten-free diet can cause more harm than good, because people may not be getting the right amounts of vitamins, minerals, and fiber.

Science has found that the only reason to avoid gluten is if you are sensitive to it, and studies suggest that about one percent of the population is. Otherwise, there's absolutely no reason to avoid it. Eating gluten-free is not healthier, though it is often perceived to be because of the benefits it has for those that are sensitive to it.

Where did it come from?

Gluten-free eating is a treatment for those with celiac disease. This type of eating was introduced in the 1950s by Dutch pediatrician Willem Karol Dicke.

In recent years, the idea of eating gluten-free has taken off, and many misunderstand it to mean healthier eating. Many brands market their products as gluten-free to customers looking to eat more healthfully. However, researchers explain that if you aren't sensitive to gluten, you're restricting your diet unnecessarily.

What are the pros and cons?

If you have celiac disease, eating gluten-free is an absolute must. If you're sensitive to gluten, cutting it out of your diet will give you some benefits, but you can't ignore the drawbacks, either.

Pros	Cons
Reverses damage to intestinal tract	Lack of fiber can cause digestive issues
Encourages label reading and food awareness	Can cause weight gain, because you might be inclined to substitute the gluten-filled products for sugar
More likely to eat less processed foods	May not receive proper nutrients

In other words, you shouldn't really be concerned about eating gluten-free unless you have a negative reaction to gluten to begin with.

What is the expected cost?

Eating gluten-free is more expensive than eating normally. One gluten-free eater explains that where she used to spend $90/week on groceries, she now spends around $130. Eating gluten-free can cost you up to twice as much as regular groceries according to the president of the National Foundation for Celiac Awareness ("A Gluten-Free Diet" 2014).

If you aren't required to eat gluten-free, don't. It will save you hassle as well as your hard-earned money.

Vegetarian/Vegan Diets

What is it?

In general, vegetarian diets mean that you exclude animal products in varying degrees from your diet. There are tons of different kinds of vegetarian diets, so let's take a look at them here.

- **You're a vegan:** you don't consume any kind of animal product, including dairy.

- **You're a lacto vegetarian:** you exclude meat products as well as eggs from your diet, but you still consume dairy products such as cheese and milk.

- **You're an ovo vegetarian:** you don't eat any kind of animal products including meat and dairy, but you do eat eggs.

- **You're a lacto-ovo vegetarian:** you don't eat meat or fish, but you do eat dairy products as well as eggs. This is the most common type of vegetarian.

- **You're a pollotarian:** you're semi-vegetarian, because you exclude all meat from your diet except poultry and fowl.

- **You're a pescatarian:** you exclude all meat products from your diet except for fish and seafood.

- **You're a flexitarian:** you eat a mostly plant-based diet, but you do eat meat every once in a while.

So, what's the point of excluding animal products from your diet? The Vegan Society breaks up the answer into four parts: for the animals, for your health, for the environment, and for people.

For the animals refers to having compassion for animals. The goal of going vegan is to help put an end to animal cruelty and exploitation.

For your health refers to the benefits you receive from eating a plant-based diet. The Vegan Society says you can reap the following benefits: increased energy, younger looking skin, and also decreased susceptibility to illnesses like obesity, heart disease, diabetes, and cancer.

For the environment refers to lowering your carbon footprint.

Finally, *for people* refers to taking a stand against "inefficient food systems," which affect the poorest people across the world.

You may be interested in all of these general benefits, but we're going to focus on "for your health." Going vegan can sometimes be horrible for your health, because many don't go the plant-based route — instead, they lean on vegan junk food, which is full of salt and sugar. They end up not getting the essential vitamins and minerals they need to survive, which can lead to terrible side effects, such as hair loss.

So, the benefits I'm about to explain are based on eating plant-based foods, not processed junk food. Vegan diets tend to be higher in fiber, which decreases the risk of cancer. Also, vegan eaters tend to eat many more fruits and vegetables than non-vegan eaters, which can reduce premature death by 33 percent (The Vegan Society).

Studies have found that, in general, vegans are leaner, they have lower BMIs, and they have lower body fat percentages than non-vegan eaters. This means that all of those weight-related diseases (diabetes, heart disease, blood pressure, and cancer) are much less likely to develop.

These are more of the long-term effects, but if you're looking for fast results, The Vegan Society talks about some quick benefits: increased energy, clearer skin, reduced allergy symptoms, stronger hair and nails, and migraine relief.

Of course, these benefits will only materialize if you're eating "green leafy vegetables, whole grains and other nutritious foods each day, including B12 fortified products" (The Vegan Society).

Where did it come from?

November 1 wasn't always World Vegan Day — so, where did the term come from? Donald Watson, the founder of The Vegan Society, first coined the term "vegan" in 1944. The word was coined from the obvious choice — vegetarian — but it was formed as a statement against traditional vegetarians who ate dairy products (Suddath 2008).

Vegetarianism has been around for a really long time, with some historians saying it dates back to Ancient Greece. However, the actual word "vegetarian" started its journey in the 1830s. The diet was mainly connected to religious organizations and beliefs.

This diet has come a really long way, with about 10 percent of the population claiming to be vegetarian, and about 1 percent of the population claiming to be strictly vegan.

What are the pros and cons?

We already looked at most of the health benefits that come along with having a plant-based diet. Not only are there health benefits, but there are environmental benefits as well. Not everyone sees the benefits of choosing this lifestyle; let's take a look at other perspectives.

First of all, about 92 percent of vegans and 47 percent of lacto-ovo vegetarians are deficient in vitamin B12, which is important in the formation of blood and the function of the brain (Dong 1982).

While The Vegan Society claims that eating vegan has many health benefits, Kris Gunnars, BSc and CEO and Founder of Authority Nutrition explains that those health benefits aren't necessarily from avoiding animal products. He explains that the studies that have been done to prove this aren't that reliable, because they are observational studies, which means they are demonstrating correlation, not causation.

He says that the correlation between health benefits and being vegan aren't necessarily because the vegans are avoiding animal products (2013): "The vegetarians are probably healthier because they are more health conscious overall, eat more vegetables, are less likely to smoke, more likely to exercise, etc. It has nothing to do with avoiding animal foods."

He says that the reason many vegans experience all these great benefits, at least in the short term before the nutrient-deficiencies kick in, is because they have taken a stance against processed, sugar-filled food. When you drastically change your eating patterns to cut out all processed junk, you will inevitably reap the short and long term benefits that The Vegan Society has cited.

Another thing that Gunnars points out is the huge difference between conventional, processed meats and unprocessed, natural meats. He explains that all of the studies that link meat eating with negative health effects are based on grain-fed, poorly treated animals, not grass-fed, free-range animals.

That's a lot to digest. Here's a quick and easy pros vs. cons chart, which will be set up as Kris Gunnars vs. The Vegan Society.

Kris Gunnars	The Vegan Society
More likely to be vitamin-deficient	Eat a variety of plants; use supplements when you need to
The studies are not controlled trials, rendering them unreliable	Studies have been done showing the positive health benefits of going vegan
Health benefits from eating vegan aren't necessarily due to avoiding animal products	Eating vegan helps to protect animals from cruel and unfair circumstances
The negative effects of processed meat are much different from the positive effects of unprocessed meat	The amount of grain needed for meat production is a significant cause of deforestation, habitat loss, and species extinction

If you do decide to go vegan, dietitians across the planet stress the importance of monitoring your vitamin and nutrient intake. If you aren't getting the proper nutrients, your body will slowly begin to shut down.

What is the expected cost?

Eating vegan doesn't have to be expensive. When people think that eating vegan is expensive, they're usually picturing the price tags that come along with faux meats and cheeses, which are pricey. If you focus on eating plants and legumes, you'll notice that you're saving a lot of money due to the lack of meat and processed foods.

Beans! Have you ever noticed how cheap beans are? You can buy dried beans for pocket change, and they're a staple in every vegan diet. Color up your cabinets with mung, kidney, cannellini, and chickpeas (just to name a few).

Always opt for fresh, whole foods. You get so much more for your money when you shop this way. Avoid the pre-packaged frozen dinners. Your wallet will thank you.

Lastly, don't think that going vegan means eating fancy foods. If you stick to the basics, you can come up with some really delicious recipes that are actually much cheaper than the meaty counterparts.

Different people have different things to say about the cost of going vegan. For Antonia Farzan, going vegan meant spending $100 more per month. However, she explains that she spends more money on things like vegan frozen pizza, vegan sour cream, and vegan ice cream, which are all pricier than their non-vegan comparables. She doesn't actually eat vegan for any of the usual reasons — she found that cutting out all animal products cleared up her cystic acne, which nothing else could cure.

On the other hand, a study published in the *Journal of Hunger & Environmental Nutrition* (2015) found that eating vegan saves you around $750 per year.

It all depends on which approach you decide to take — a plant-based approach or a processed foods approach.

The Raw Foods Diet

What is it?

According to Kristina Carillo Bucaram, founder of FullyRaw, the basis of the raw foods diet is eating your food completely raw. Big surprise, right? She explains: "A raw foods diet is made up of fresh, whole, unrefined, living, plant-based foods: fruits, vegetables, leafy greens, nuts, and seeds, which are consumed in their natural state, without cooking or steaming."

This is what you would be consuming on the raw foods diet:

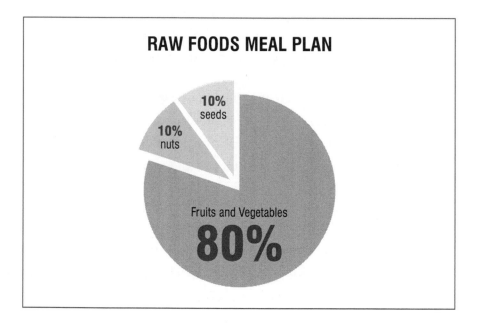

People that eat this way are called "raw fooders" or "raw vegans." Since you're eating only raw foods, you can guess that you won't be eating any meat. Bucaram explains that you get all of your calories from fruits and vegetables with a small emphasis on nuts and seeds.

So, what's the point? Bucaram says that a lot of the food we eat has toxic residue on it, which our bodies are forced to deal with. When you eat raw food, you cleanse your body of those chemicals. Another great effect of eating raw food is that you won't experience constipation or bad gas: " [...] the transit time of waste matter shortens to 24 hours or less, avoiding the buildup of toxemia from the recycling of toxins from the colon."

The other big question is: what's wrong with cooked food? We've been cooking our food for a really long time, so why ditch the stovetop now? Bucaram explains that when you heat your food, you're actually damaging the nutrients it contains. This isn't a new find either — dieticians and researchers have been talking about this for a long time.

When you eat cooked foods, your body reacts the same way it does to foreign pathogens like bacteria and viruses. Cooking food does the following:

- Denatures the proteins
- Carcinogizes the fats
- Caramelizes the carbohydrates
- Damages and destroys nutrients
- Leaves you with empty calories, which enlarges your pancreas

The argument is that cooked food is not natural food — it alters the food's original and best state, leaving you with a product that is less than ideal. Bucaram even goes so far as to say that cooked food is the cause of cancer, heart disease, and diabetes.

On the other side of the argument, we have people like Matt Fitzgerald (he showed up earlier in the book — he's the author of "Diet Cults"), who says that all this talk about damaging food when it's cooked is bologna (for lack of a better word). He explains, "[…] It is not necessary to avoid cooked foods generally to keep the intake of the most harmful cooking-related toxins within safe limits."

He goes on to say that experts agree about the effect of cooked foods on our body: "Experts agree that a diet which includes few fried foods and an otherwise normal mix of cooked and raw foods will not shorten life by the sort of poisoning that raw-foodists fear."

However, raw foodists continue to preach the importance of eating food the "natural" and "clean" way.

Making the switch from mostly cooked food to raw food is super hard, and it discourages a lot of people from even trying. A lot of people start to miss the additives we're used to like salt and sugars, but Bucaram says that time is the key: "Once the taste buds are no longer exposed each day to these 'excitotoxins,' they once again develop an appreciation for the taste of sweet, fresh fruits and vegetables."

Like any diet out there, you have to give your taste buds time to go from the excitement of all the fake stuff out there to the reality of fresh, real food.

Where did it come from?

Well, many argue that the raw foods diet is the oldest diet around, because that is how food was eaten before we mastered fire. That makes it difficult to fully explain where this diet came from, but it started to gain popularity in 1930, when Dr. Paul Kouchakoff found that eating cooked foods wasn't ideal.

Chris Carlton and Kira Goldy, creators of the site Purely Raw, explain how the history of raw food progressed. In 1966, A. Hovannessian published "Raw Eating" in Iran. By about 1975, this diet started to grow in the states with several publications on the topic, and today, there are even restaurants dedicated to serving gourmet raw food.

The movement is spiraling, with people claiming that it can cure incurable diseases among a ton of other health benefits.

What are the pros and cons?

If going vegan seems too hard for you, then this diet might be out of reach. This is veganism on steroids, because not only are you cutting out animal products, but you aren't allowed to cook what you *can* eat. If you find that you often struggle with willpower and challenges, this diet might end up just bringing you down in the long run.

If you're up for the challenge, then this diet can bring you a ton of health benefits, even if you only do it for a short period of time. If you're interested in cutting out the toxins of junk food, you might consider doing the raw foods diet for 30 days.

Here is a chart with some pros and cons if you're considering taking on this hard-core diet.

Pros	Cons
Cleanses your body of toxins	Cleansing foods aren't anabolic foods, meaning they don't rebuild new tissues very well; you can't cleanse forever
Connects you closely with nature	You will likely need to take many supplements due to a lack of zinc, iron, and vitamin B12
You get to keep the nutrients in your food that cooking often destroys	Cooking can destroy harmful bacteria, and in some cases, it actually makes antioxidants more potent
Lowers risk of heart disease, diabetes, and cancer	You spend a lot of time chewing
Weight loss	Food choices are very limited due to lack of cooking

There are a lot of questions that people have about the raw foods diet; to get more information, you can visit **www.fullyraw.com**.

The raw foods diet is something that all animals do — humans are the only species that cooks. If you want to get closer to nature and reap some of the benefits at the same time, the raw foods diet might be a good place for you to start.

What is the expected cost?

Most advocates of the raw foods diet say that buying organic is a must. If you can't afford to go organic, you can meet halfway and purchase organic for only the dirty dozen. Organic food is more expensive than traditional produce, so you will naturally be spending more money.

The upside is that you aren't buying any meat products, which are usually the most expensive thing in your shopping cart.

You can spend as little as $3.33 per day if you follow Melody Polakow's meal plan from her blog MeloMeals (**http://melomeals.blogspot.com**).

How much you spend is entirely reliant on how much preparation you do, where you grocery shop, and how much organic produce you are willing to buy.

The Daniel Plan

What is it?

If you're religious and want to lose weight, The Daniel Plan might be for you. The goal of this plan is to start a healthier lifestyle through the use of faith and friends. The "Daniel" part comes from the biblical figure, Daniel, who rejected the king's rich food in order to honor God.

The idea behind this plan is this: "With the support of God and your group, you have far more than willpower helping you to make positive changes so you can be consistent and sustain your new healthy lifestyle."

The idea is to use God and friends to keep you accountable in your trek to health. There are basically three steps to the plan:

1. Create an online profile.
2. Read the book that goes along with the diet: "The Daniel Plan: 40 Days to a Healthier Life."
3. Start a small group and get the 6-week study to do together.

The foundational scripture that goes along with the plan is from 1 Corinthians 10:31. "So whether you eat or drink, or whatever you do, do it all for the glory of God."

As far as the actual diet goes, the foods on your plate are split up like this:

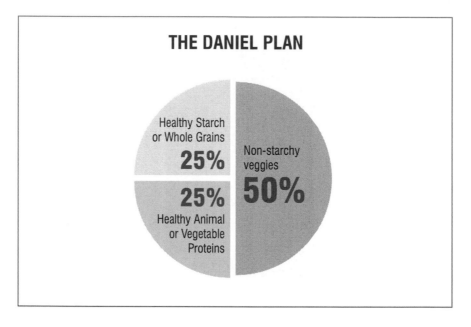

Then on the side, you're supposed to have some low-glycemic fruit, and you're allowed to drink water or herbal iced teas.

The diet itself is very wholesome and doesn't really cut out any of the major food groups. If you want to see the approved foods list, visit **https://danielplan.com/healthyhabits/shoppinglist**.

Where did it come from?

Pastor Rick Warren was baptizing a huge group of people one day (over 800 people), and he realized something a little disheartening. Most of them were overweight (himself included!). One week later, he stood in front of his congregation and asked everyone to forgive him for being a "poor steward of his health" (The Daniel Plan).

He asked everyone if they'd like to join him on a quest to being healthy, and over 12,000 people signed up alongside him. He teamed up with three doctors (including Dr. Oz) and created this easy-to-follow program.

What are the pros and cons?

This plan isn't nearly as talked about as programs like Weight Watchers or Atkins, but the people who have used the program have experienced great results. The first year of The Daniel Plan (2011) helped over 15,000 people collectively lose over 250,000 pounds. People from over 190 countries have participated in the relatively new program.

The reason this has been so successful for people is because it isn't just about food — it's about becoming healthier in many aspects of life (mind, body, and spirit).

Here are some of the pros and cons to the diet:

Pros	Cons
You don't need to count calories	You have to purchase materials to get started
Weight loss	You aren't supposed to do this diet alone; it's designed for groups
Addresses you as a whole, not just food or exercise	The diet is relatively new; there aren't many studies, and there isn't an app to go along with the website
Simple and easy to follow — the methods used are tried-and-true for losing weight	The program is more of a guideline; it leaves a lot of the planning up to you

In general, the cons aren't that extreme — this method of eating isn't controversial. There are no major food groups left out, and there is no reason to believe that you might be missing out on any of the important vitamins or nutrients that certain foods provide.

If you like the concept of this diet, but aren't so hot on the Bible study part, you can always use the approved foods list on The Daniel Plan site as a guideline for yourself.

What is the expected cost?

The cost of The Daniel Plan book is around $10. The cost of the devotional is about $12. So, just to properly begin this diet, you'll be spending between $20-$25. After that initial investment, all you have to worry about is the cost of groceries.

There is no special cost associated with the approved foods list. These are all basic food ingredients that you might already be buying. You can expect your grocery bill to be about the same as it is now.

The Mediterranean Diet

What is it?

This diet is based on what people ate in countries surrounding the Mediterranean Sea (like Italy and Greece) back in 1960. Researchers noticed how incredibly healthy these people were, so they studied their diet and came up with what we now call The Mediterranean Diet.

Here's what the food breakdown is:

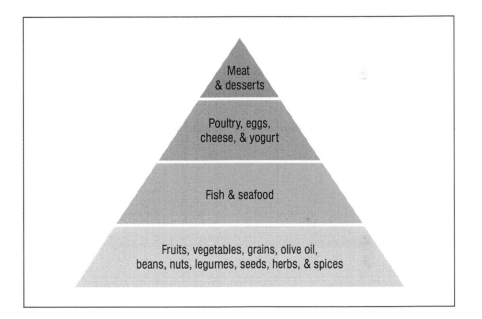

The idea is to base every meal off of the bottom bar, and to eat meat and desserts very rarely.

You might be noticing a trend here, but to effectively follow this diet, you cut out the following foods:

- Sugary drinks
- Added sugars
- Processed meat
- Refined grains and oils
- Processed foods

All of the diets that we have looked at have made a point to steer you away from sugar and processed foods.

Some examples of approved foods would be vegetables like broccoli and spinach, fruits like bananas and oranges, nuts and seeds like almonds and pumpkin seeds, legumes like peas and lentils, and tubers like sweet potatoes and turnips. To see more food options, you can visit **https:// authoritynutrition.com/mediterranean-diet-meal-plan**.

Where did it come from?

We kind of already covered this in the previous section, but this diet came from researchers noticing how healthy people living around the Mediterranean are. According to one of the leading Mediterranean diet researchers, Antonia Trichopoulou, this diet has evolved over the course of 5,000 years (qtd. in Palmer 2013).

Researchers have studied this diet across the world for over 50 years now, and hundreds of studies have shown the amazing health benefits. In comparison to the American Heart Association recommended diet, which is very low in fat, this high-fat diet has actually done better in terms of heart health. The risk of cardiovascular disease actually decreased by 30 percent and the risk of stroke decreased by almost 50 percent.

What are the pros and cons?

There is no question that this diet has incredible results on health, particularly heart health. The diet isn't necessarily meant for weight loss, but those who start eating this way do find that their extra fat starts to melt off.

Another perk of the diet is that red wine isn't only allowed — it's encouraged. You should obviously not drink if you aren't 21 yet, but it's definitely something to look forward to.

Pros	Cons
Reduces risk for heart disease, strokes, diabetes, Alzheimer's disease, Parkinson's disease, and premature death	May be more expensive
Weight loss	Cooking fresh food is time consuming
You are encouraged to drink one glass of red wine per day	Exact serving amounts aren't clear; calorie totals aren't stated

What is the expected cost?

The cost of this diet can get expensive, but many stress the importance of being budget-conscious. Studies show that this diet isn't necessarily the most expensive diet out there, but it does cost more than the SAD.

The estimated cost of the typical American diet is about $10 per day. The Mediterranean diet edges toward the $16 mark, according to Katherine Hobson of US News & World Report (Forte 2010).

One thing that number doesn't show, though, is the savings on medical expenses due to the reduced risk for all those diseases mentioned above. In the long run, the investment in your food will pay for itself 10 times over.

Some other tips are to buy less meat and to only splurge on high-quality olive oil, fresh herbs, fresh greens, and fruits. You can generally find olive oil in bulk, which can be a money saver. To read more on how to save money while on this diet, visit **www.mediterraneanbook. com/2010/02/27/cost-eat-mediterranean**.

Cleanses

You've made it — go ahead and breathe a sigh of earned relief. This is the last diet we'll be looking at in this book. I shouldn't say diet, because cleanses are generally very short-term. You can pair a cleanse with one of the other diets/lifestyles mentioned above, or you might notice that some of those diets have a temporary cleanse built-in.

What is it?

So, what is a cleanse? Sometimes people refer to cleanses as "detoxes," but the concept is the same across the board. This short-term lifestyle reboot is meant to clean out your system and jump-start your body for a more active, healthier life. The goal is to drink a ton of juice, which pushes all of the chemicals and toxins out of your body.

If you find that you feel congested or you've eaten a ton of not-so-great food, a weekend cleanse might be the answer for you.

There is no single way to juice — different companies and sources have different suggestions, but all of the cleanses are based on drinking liquid only for a certain period of time.

Here are some popular cleansing options:

Urban Remedy (**www.urbanremedy.com**) suggests a three part process: pre-cleanse, during, and post-cleanse. During the pre-cleanse, you're supposed to drink eight glasses of water per day and eliminate all of the bad stuff from your diet. During the cleanse, you start your day with a glass of water garnished with a lemon, and then you drink six juices per day in 2 hour increments. The post-cleanse is basically adding food back into your diet.

This diet is pretty (when I say pretty, I mean extremely) expensive, as they provide the juices for you, and you have to buy them. You can cleanse anywhere from 3-30 days, and the price is $74.99 per day. Yes, per day. That means that if you want to cleanse for one month, you can expect to pay over $2,000.

You can obviously take the concept of this cleanse and make the juices yourself if you want to, but the ease and readiness of the juices won't be there.

A similar cleanse done by a different company, BluePrint (**www.blueprint.com**), offers basically the same thing as Urban Remedy — 6 juices per day — for $65. Though this cleanse is cheaper, the price adds up really fast. That $16 per day Mediterranean diet isn't looking so bad now, is it?

There are other companies that do juice cleanses, too, such as Life Juice, Cooler Cleanse, Liquiteria, Organic Avenue, and Ritual Cleanse.

There are also green cleanses, which are focused on replacing your meals with vibrantly green juice concoctions.

If you don't have the means to buy a pre-made cleanse, you can consider whipping up your own juice blends. Health.com has some good recipes in their article "7 Nutrition-Rich Juice Recipes." You can always turn to Pinterest for cleansing tips, too.

Where did it come from?

Who the heck came up with this? We were wondering the same thing. Apparently it's been around for just about as long as humans have. Detoxification expert, Brenda Watson, explains that it dates back to 2700 BC with the Chinese. She says, "All cultures have traditionally used eliminative herbs that have laxative, diuretic, and blood purifying properties to remove toxins from the body" (2012).

People have cleansed using a ton of different methods. People still do these things, but as far as cleansing in the eating and dieting sense goes, juicing is usually the preferred method.

What are the pros and cons?

While a cleanse can be a great boost to a healthy lifestyle, it's recommended that you don't do it for longer than three days. Here are some of the pros and cons.

Pros	Cons
Gets rid of toxins in the body, making you feel pretty amazing	Experts argue that our bodies are capable of detoxifying themselves
Bad habits can shift with the help of a cleanse	You shouldn't expect any long-lasting weight loss
You will rid your body of excess water weight	You aren't getting enough fat and protein, which leads to some nasty side effects (dizziness, headaches, and fatigue)

In general, the nasty side effects are going to happen if you do the cleanse for too long. If you only cleanse for two to three days, it should give you the maximum reward with the least amount of negative side effects.

What is the expected cost?

We broke down the cost of doing a pre-established juice cleanse, but even making the juices yourself is going to be pricey. The biggest cost is going to be getting a juicer, which can be more expensive than the actual cleanse you're going to do (prices range between a few hundred dollars to over a grand).

Even the most cost-savvy of bloggers could only get the cost down to about $30 per day (**www.andherlittledogtoo.com**).

If you're doing it short-term, the cost won't be so bad, but even $60 (the cheapest possible 2-day cleanse) is a pretty penny to spend.

Especially when you're a poor college student — let's get real.

CASE STUDY: LAURIE BEEBE, MS, RD

Diet Coach, Owner of Shaping Your Future
www.mycoachlaurie.com

Laurie Beebe said that students have so many new responsibilities that they frequently put nutrition too far down on their list of priorities. She realizes that students often socialize around food and may also turn to food for comfort when feeling homesick or to cope with new stressors.

Beebe suggests that learning to cook a little bit and maintaining a regular eating pattern will help you to achieve success. She reminds us all to incorporate exercise into our daily routines.

When Beebe was in college, she was part of a group of students who prepared meals together, taking turns to buy food, cook, and clean up. She suggests posting a notice on the dorm bulletin board that expresses an interest in starting a small group of three or four people to share dinner three or four nights per week.

Beebe's advice to students is:

1. Eat three meals a day and limit "treats" (like candy bars from vending machines, late-night eating, and high-calorie fast foods) to just one instance every other day or so.

2. Find something you like that you can have for breakfast, no matter how much you are in a hurry, to start your metabolism going and stave off late-day hunger.

3. Get in plenty of walking for exercise if you do not have a regular exercise routine.

"I would teach students that for every extra 100 calories they eat in a day, this can add up to gaining a pound at the end of the month. So, if they do not want to go home with an extra five pounds at the end of the semester, keep an eye on those extras/treats/junk foods, and just say 'no' once in a while," she said.

*A registered dietitian for more than 25 years, Beebe became certified in Adult Weight Management in 2006, and then completed the core essential coaching courses at Coach U in 2007. Her mission is to help people lose weight permanently by making small changes, one at a time, to develop lasting, healthy habits. Beebe's Web site is **www.mycoachlaurie.com**, and she hosts two blogs to provide you with weight loss tips (**http://lifedietbalance.blogspot.com**) and nutrition information (**http://askthedietitian.blogspot.com**).*

CHAPTER 4

Eating on a Budget

Here's the elephant in the room.

Sure, eating healthy sounds great, but I'm broke.

Well, the reality of life is that the only things you absolutely need to survive are food and shelter. So, it only makes sense that the two things at the top of your budgeting list would be just that — the cost of your living quarters (probably your dorm or apartment) and your groceries.

So, when you're creating your budget, make sure that you're prioritizing. If you're living off your parent's help, this won't be an issue for you, but if you're living off your savings or a part-time job, it's important that you're setting money aside for your food.

If you're eating out a lot, you're spending more money than you should be. If you're buying too much produce at a time, you might find that things spoil before you get to it, which is costing you money.

Sketching out a budget for your food is an important first step. Once you know how much money you have to spend on food, you can determine where to begin.

Where to Start

When it comes to buying food, there are a lot of options — almost too many options. Where do you go and how do you make the best choice? Let's take a look at what you're dealing with, and we'll evaluate all the options.

The dorm or apartment kitchen

Now is the time to look around your kitchen. See whether you have a dedicated kitchen sink, a refrigerator, a freezer compartment, a stove, a microwave, cabinets or shelves, and counter space. The more of these you have, the more cooking you can do for yourself. It's also important to know the facility rules for your living arrangement. If you aren't sure, find out whether you can have a hot plate (if needed) and a small indoor grilling machine.

If you do have the ability to cook for yourself, you're already at a huge advantage. The main issue with going out to eat or even eating at the dining halls is that you don't know what's being used to create your food. Often times, other places will prepare food with cheap oils, extra salt, and added sugars. When you cook at home, you have the ability to choose what kinds of oils you're using, you can regulate the salt you add, and you can cut out those extra sugars in a conscious way.

It's a lot easier to count your macros when you're preparing your own food. However, you might not have that option if you're living in a dorm without a kitchen or a space to cook.

Dining halls

You need to make a simple evaluation. Is the food available to you through the cafeteria basically healthy or unhealthy? Are good choices available all day long? Is it open for three meals a day, or early morning until late night? Is it open all weekend? These answers will help you determine how often you wish to cook for yourself.

If you don't have the option to cook for yourself, you'll have to work with what the dining hall has to offer. All dining halls do have healthy options; it's very likely that the loaded mac and cheese, the French fries, and the dessert buffet are blinding you. When there's always hot and ready food that's loaded with sugar and processed ingredients, it can be hard to stay on the right path.

You're going to have to rely on your willpower to get through it. If you have an organized way of tracking what you eat, it can actually make the temptation a lot easier to resist. By "organized way of tracking what you eat," I mean a way of counting your calories or your macros. If you're keeping track of those, you'll quickly realize that the one serving of mac and cheese is enough calories to cover your breakfast, lunch, and part of your dinner — it'll open your eyes to the death trap of the dining hall.

Grocery stores

What mode of transportation do you have? If you have a car, shopping will be a lot easier. If you use public transportation, ride a bike, or walk, you will need to get precise about the location of the stores and where you can feasibly travel to each week. The number of groceries you can carry will naturally limit you.

Convenience stores

Convenience stores are bad choices for buying groceries. They generally charge much more, and they don't have as many healthy choices like fresh fruits and vegetables. Don't fall into the trap of shopping at them on a regular basis just because they're closer or are open during certain hours. Plan your trips, and go to a traditional, discount, or bulk grocery store instead.

Traditional stores

Traditional grocery stores are perfect places to buy your weekly groceries. Find out where the stores are located around you, and go with the closest proximity unless one has significantly lower prices. Your parents will generally know which stores have the most economical prices.

Discount stores

These are frequently small grocery stores with good prices, limited produce, and all-generic products. They can be an excellent place to buy eggs, milk, bread, coffee, soup, and many other basic items. Experimentation will tell whether you like the kinds of items they offer. The paper products are generally not that great.

Many of the food items, such as pies and biscuits may be made with a lot of processed ingredients as well as added sugars — stay away from them. The cereals also might not be whole grain. If you shop at these stores, you may need to make a second stop at a produce market or a traditional store to buy more fruits and vegetables as well as products that are wholesome as opposed to processed.

Bulk stores

Whether you should shop at bulk stores depends on several factors, such as whether you have a car to get the large items home and the space to store large quantities. If you have both, you still need to be careful that the prices are indeed lower. Only buy bulk items that will not go bad in six months or so, such as toilet tissue, paper towels, cleaners, canned goods, and some boxed items.

If you live in a dorm with roommates, this can be a great option for everyone to chip in on. You can split the cost of the membership fee, and you can buy bulk items for everyone. You can all split the cost of these items and then have days where you cook for everyone. This can be a dream or a nightmare depending on who your roommates are. If you decide to do this, make sure you split up all the money before you go. Otherwise, you might find that you just paid for everyone's groceries.

Eating Out

Sometimes you don't want to eat at the dining hall, you don't have time to cook, and you're out of groceries. It happens. In that case, you'll probably find yourself going somewhere and placing an order or ordering some kind of take out.

Before we get into how to make the best choice, there's the question of cost. According to Joel Runyon, founder of the Ultimate Paleo Guide, the cost of eating out is insane when you actually break it down.

Eating Out one meal a day: **$450/month**

- $15/meal
- 30 meals/month
- $450/month

Eating Out two meals a day: **$900/month**

- $15/meal
- 60 meals/month
- $900/month

These figures aren't even assuming that you do spend some money on groceries here and there.

If you buy groceries instead, you can expect to spend about **$300/ month**. The USDA has a chart that comes out each month providing the previous month's figures on how much you should be spending on groceries. Here's the February 2016 chart broken down, only showing the figures for the monthly budget of a single male or female between 19-50 years old.

	Thrifty plan	Low-cost plan	Moderate-cost plan	Liberal plan
Male	$189	$244.10	$305.70	$376.20
Female	$166.80	$211.70	$261.50	$333.40

This graph is assuming that you are eating at home for each meal.

If you do decide that you have some extra money in your budget to eat out, maybe even just once in a while, there are some things to consider. You need to determine which restaurants are available to you given your transportation constraints. Is takeout available? Do they charge for delivery? Can you order takeout with friends or roommates? Do these restaurants have healthy menu options that you like?

Eating out can be a huge help when you need it, but you need to make sure you're choosing a place that brags about its healthy options. Chinese takeout is often loaded with heavy oils and added sugars, Mexican options can be loaded with salt, and All-American buffets are full of processed carbs. You can generally find healthy options everywhere, but know that you won't always be aware of what ingredients are hiding in your food.

Look for keywords such as grilled, baked, or steamed, and browse the menu for a "healthy options" or a "lite fare" section. The big thing you want to avoid is fried food. Not only will it clog up your body with extra oils (often times, it's very cheap oil that's being used, such as beef tallow), but it'll also make your body very unhappy. You'll notice your skin breaking out, your stomach bloating, and maybe even some headaches coming on.

There are sites all over the Internet that will give you the best options depending on what restaurant you're going to. You can also request a nutrition information sheet to calculate the macros you're eating. The only thing is that there probably isn't going to be an ingredients list, so it's harder to know exactly what's going into your body.

Organic vs. Regular Food Cost

So, we already know that organic food is pricier than regular food — or is it?

It seems like a given that organic options are more expensive than their traditional counterparts, but a study done by Consumer Reports revealed that this isn't always the case. The study compared 100 different products at eight different grocers across the country. They found that the following organic products were actually the same price or cheaper than the regular ones (2015):

- Honey (as much as 13 percent cheaper)
- Lettuce
- Carrots
- Maple syrup
- Olive oil
- Cream cheese

While these products were sometimes cheaper, we would be foolish to think that all organic products are the same price or cheaper — they definitely aren't. The same study found that products like zucchini are up to 303 percent more expensive.

Here are some quick comparisons:

Regular apples (lb.)	$1.66
Organic apples (lb.)	$2.00
% Difference	**+20%**

Regular beef (85% lean ground, lb.)	$4.99
Organic beef (85% lean ground, lb.)	$8.63
% Difference	**+73%**

Regular eggs (large brown, dozen)	$3.59
Organic eggs (large brown, dozen)	$5.69
% Difference	**+58%**

In general, the organic stuff is going to cost more because of its higher quality and more difficult farming methods. If you are going to splurge on organic foods — and eight out of every 10 households do — you should focus on fresh foods like fruits, vegetables, and meat. In general, you won't get the best bang for your buck when you splurge on processed organic food like chips and cookies.

For a guideline on breaking down the fresh food categories even more, see the Dirty Dozen and Clean Fifteen lists in Chapter 2.

CASE STUDY: NICOLE BRITVAN, RD, CDE

Nutritionist, Certified Diabetes
Educator
San Francisco, CA
Telephone: 415-722-2616

Nicole Britvan thinks students should not overlook the importance of at least seven hours of sleep each night, as a lack of adequate sleep can lead to weight gain. She reminds us that liquid calories add up quickly and to be mindful of what our body needs versus what it wants. Britvan encourages students to aim for at least 30 minutes of exercise each day. She has noted in her practice that when we are stressed, we crave fat, salt, and sugar. Her top advice to students is:

1. Water (plain or sparkling) — make it your main beverage. An extra 100 calories a day is 10 lbs. of weight gain in one year — this is easy to do with juice, energy drinks, and other sugary drinks.

2. Eat fruit and vegetables whenever possible.

3. Be careful about late-night eating due to stress, anxiety, or boredom.

CHAPTER 5

Reading the Labels

Labels are one of the most important things to understand when it comes to eating healthfully. The sad thing is that they're also really tricky to decipher. Companies want you to keep buying their products, but if everyone could really see what the product is, they might not want to eat it so much.

This chapter will help you understand everything about labeling, from the ingredients section to those marketing terms on the front of the product.

Ingredient Labels

This is a great place to start, because it's arguably one of the most important parts of the label. The ingredients in the item are more important than the macronutrients (the nutrition facts). Here's why.

One medium-sized apple has 19 grams of sugar in it. It's not added or anything, it's just part of the natural fruit. Now, that sugar isn't necessarily bad for you. It digests more slowly through your system, so the fructose takes a while to hit your liver. Your body is more likely to use this sugar for fuel more quickly than say, table sugar, which means the sugar is turned into energy rather than fat.

On the other hand, let's say there's some kind of processed food that also contains 19 grams of sugar, but the first ingredient in the ingredients list is sugar. That's not a natural sugar. It's going to hit your liver quickly, and you won't feel nearly as full as you would if you'd eaten an apple.

Beyond that fact, the ingredients trump any marketing tools being used on the product. For example (and we'll get into this later on this chapter), the label on the front of the product might brag that it's "low-fat" or "natural" or "organic," but these terms are very wide-ranging, and sometimes they don't really mean anything at all. Don't be fooled by the marketing labels — rely on the ingredients list to shine light on what you're actually consuming.

Moral of the story is that the ingredients are the most important part of your labels.

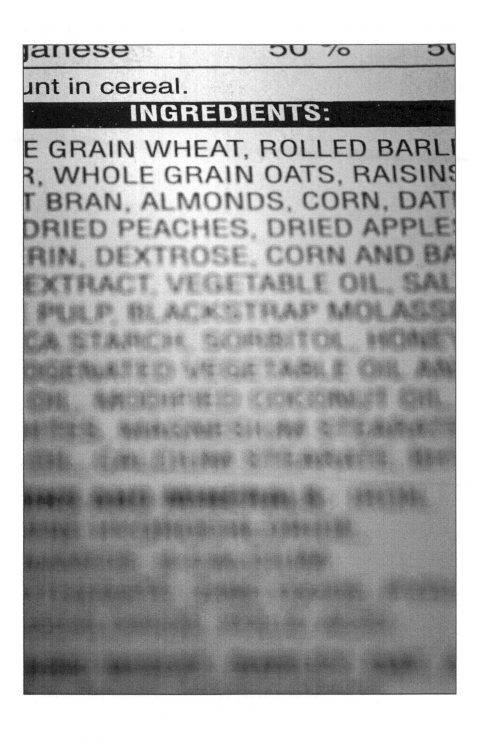

janese 50 % 5(

unt in cereal.

INGREDIENTS:

E GRAIN WHEAT, ROLLED BARLI
R, WHOLE GRAIN OATS, RAISIN:
T BRAN, ALMONDS, CORN, DAT
DRIED PEACHES, DRIED APPLE
RIN, DEXTROSE, CORN AND B/
EXTRACT, VEGETABLE OIL, SAL
PULP, BLACKSTRAP MOLAS:
CA STARCH, SORBITOL, HONE
DGENATED VEGETABLE OIL, AI
OIL, MODIFIED COCONUT OIL

The order of the list

Most people are aware of the significance of the order of the list, but let's make sure we cover all the bases. The order of the list correlates to the weight of the ingredient in the product. For example, if the first ingredient is "corn flour," then that means that the product has a heavy weight of corn flour in it. If the last ingredient is "sugar," than the product may have a very light amount of sugar in it. The confusing thing about this is that while the word "sugar" may be the last word in the ingredients list, it may not mean that there is a low amount of sugar in the product.

There are often times words in the list that are nearly impossible to understand. There are really long words that mean different things, and sometimes those long words are just another term for "sugar." So, be mindful when you're reading the ingredients list. Look for words that you're familiar with.

Keep reading to find out what those different scientific terms mean.

What those "long words" mean

You may be familiar with different kinds of ingredients. You may have heard that those words ending in "-ose" generally refer to sugars. For example, "sucrose" is another word for sugar.

Here are all of the most common terms that you're likely to find on your ingredient lists:

The "term"	What it really is
Brown sugar	Sugar
Corn sweetener	Sugar
Corn syrup	Sugar
Fruit juice concentrate	Sugar
High-fructose corn syrup	Sugar
Honey	Sugar
Invert sugar	Sugar
Malt sugar	Sugar
Molasses	Sugar
Raw sugar	Sugar
Dextrose, Fructose, Glucose, Lactose, Maltose, and Sucrose	Sugar
Syrup	Sugar
Sodium bicarbonate	Salt
Sodium nitrate	Salt
Sodium citrate	Salt
Monosodium glutamate (MSG)	Salt
Sodium benzoate	Salt
Potassium sorbate	Preservative
Ascorbic acid	Preservative that prevents spoiling or loss of color
Alpha-tocopherol	Preservative that prevents spoiling or loss of color
Any phrase containing word "butylated"	Preservative that prevents spoiling or loss of color
Sulfite or sulfur terms	Preservative that prevents bacterial and fungal growth

The "term"	What it really is
Proprionic acid	Preservative that prevents mold growth in baked goods like bread
Nitrates	Preservative that prevents bacterial growth
Any phrase containing words sorbate and benzoate	Preservative that prevents bacterial growth
Castoreum	Augments vanilla and strawberry flavorings; comes from rendered beaver anal glands
Cochineal extract	Color additive; comes from insect shells
Synthetic colors	Made from petroleum
Isoeugenol	Adds a spice flavor similar to nutmeg
Niacin	Vitamin B3
Folic acid	B vitamin
Beta-carotene	Red-orange pigment to preserve color

The list of color additives is so long that I can't include it in this book. Know that any label such as "Red 40," "Blue 1," or "Yellow 6" denotes a color that is added to your food product. To see the full list of acceptable and restricted color additives, visit **www.fda.gov/ForIndustry/ColorAdditives/ColorAdditiveInventories/ucm106626.htm**.

There a ton of ingredients out there, and these are just some of the main ones you'll see. However, if you pick up an item and see an ingredient that you're not sure about, do a quick Internet search, and you should be able to read up on it.

Nutrition Labels

You may have had a crash course or two on how to read a nutrition label, but they can still be confusing. Let's take a more detailed look at percentages and serving sizes.

Percentages

If you've ever seen a nutritional label, you may have noticed that there are some percentages tacked on the right-hand side. Those can be slightly confusing, but the FDA explains on their site what exactly those numbers mean.

Those percentages are the Percent Daily Values (%DV). These are recommendations on how much of each nutrient you should eat based on a 2,000 calorie per day diet. You may or may not count your calories, and you might not have the caloric goal of 2,000 per day. Maybe you need more like 2,500 or maybe you're more comfortable around 1,700.

In those cases, the %DV may not be as helpful, but it can still show you if a certain product is rather high in a certain nutrient. In general, a nutrient that is less than 5%DV is low. A nutrient that is higher than 20%DV is high.

The FDA says that the main goal of the %DVs is to help you compare different brands. If one brand has a product with a 33%DV when it comes to sodium, and another brand is selling the same product with a 10%DV, it can help you make the most informed decision.

If you aren't so sure what the number of grams or milligrams means, this tool can help simplify that for you by giving you a general idea of just how much that nutrient is worth.

Nutrition Facts

Serving Size 1 cup (200g)
Servings per Container 4

Amount Per Serving	
Calories 300	Calories from Fat 110

	% Daily Value
Total Fat 12g	20%
Saturated Fat 4g	22%
Cholesterol 0mg	0%
Sodium 70mg	6%
Total Carbohydrate 30g	10%
Dietary Fiber 0g	0%
Sugars 20g	
Protein 5g	

Vitamin A 5%	Vitamin C 0%
Calcium 10%	Iron 0%

* Percent Daily Values are based on a 2,000 calorie diet.

Note that there are currently no %DVs for trans fat, sugar, and protein. This is because there is currently no established daily recommendation. In the case of protein, there isn't a %DV because, according to experts, consuming a lot of it isn't a public health concern. You can read more at **www.fda.gov**.

Serving sizes

This is the most important thing to look at when you're evaluating food products. Let's say you buy a bottle of soda. The nutrition label says the bottle has 150 calories in it. That's not too bad — right?

What if the bottle was broken down into three servings? That means that the single bottle of soda actually has 450 calories in it. Let's be real here — who is going to drink one third of a bottle of soda?

So, when you look at a product, it's important to first see how many servings are in the package. You need to evaluate how much you're expecting to eat so that you can actually see how potentially bad the product is for your body.

If the serving size is for two cookies and you know very well that you're probably going to eat the whole row, you might consider putting it back on the shelf.

Packaging

Marketing terms

Marketing terms and phrases can be very confusing. What exactly does "organic" or "natural" mean? We're all confused, so here's the low-down on those keywords on your food's packaging.

Marketing term or phrase	What it actually means
100 percent organic	Made of all organic ingredients
Organic	95 percent of the product is organic
Made with organic ingredients	70 percent of the product is organic
All natural	No added colors, artificial flavors, or "synthetic substances" (note that ingredients like high fructose corn syrup do not fall under these categories, so they would be allowed)
Sugar-free	Less than 0.5 grams of sugar
Reduced sugar or less sugar	At least 25 percent less sugar than the standard
No added sugars or without added sugars	No sugar or sugar-containing ingredients are added during processing
Low sugar	Not defined or allowed as a claim on food labels
Sodium-free	Less than 5 milligrams of sodium
Very low sodium	35 milligrams or less per serving
Low-sodium	140 milligrams or less per serving
Reduced (or less) sodium	At least 25 percent less sodium than the standard

Marketing term or phrase	What it actually means
Light (for sodium-reduced products)	If the food is "low calorie" and "low fat" and sodium is reduced by 50 percent per serving
Light in sodium	At least 50 percent less sodium than the standard

These are some of the common claims that food labels show, so at least you have an idea of what they really mean.

CASE STUDY: ELIZABETH DEROBERTIS, MS, RD, CDN, CDE

Registered Dietitian, Certified Diabetes Educator
Scarsdale Medical Group, Scarsdale
New York
www.nutritionistliz.com

Elizabeth DeRobertis says that college students need to make healthy eating a priority. She believes in starting each day with a balanced breakfast, even if it means grabbing a granola or cereal-type bar and a piece of fruit on your way out the door. She encourages us to get eight hours of sleep each night.

DeRobertis sees students eat in response to stress — she says they obtain high-calorie snacks from vending machines and go too long without eating. She would like to see a short, healthy cooking class added to school orientations and recipe cards being made available year-round. DeRobertis' advice to students includes:

1. Keep tabs on your calorie intake and prioritize where you want to spend your calories. I often think of the analogy between calories and money. Just like college kids need to be mindful of how and when they spend money, they should use the same strategic thinking when deciding how and where to spend their calories. They should look up the calorie and fat content of the foods they commonly eat if they do not have a nutrition label. Most restaurants offer their calories online. It is important not to drink empty calories. Juice, soda, Gatorade®, Vitamin Water®, and high-calorie, sugared coffee drinks can contribute hundreds of extra calories to the day, and many unwanted pounds to their waistlines.

2. Choose deli sandwiches more often than other types of "fast food" choices. Stock up on lean cold cuts, such as turkey, ham, roast beef, and chicken. This will always be fewer calories than a hamburger and fries or a piece of pizza. Buy low-fat

condiments, so if they make things like a standard tuna sand-wich, the calories and fat will be less if it is made with low-fat or fat-free mayo.

3. Start as many meals as possible with a big salad or a broth-based soup. This will help with portion control and to meet nutrient needs. I read a story once about a freshman starting college who wanted to lose weight. He made a point of having a big salad each time he entered the cafeteria, and then he let himself eat what he wanted after he finished his salad. He lost 50 pounds his first year in college by doing this.

CHAPTER 6

———— 🍴-🍽-🍷 ————

Eating for Your Brain

Maintaining a healthy lifestyle in college is tricky. Between going to class, studying, and working part-time job, eating healthy might be the last thing on your mind. But that's just it: you are — or will be — a college student. Most of your day-to-day activities involve learning and studying, and your brain is the functioning cog that makes you do those things successfully.

Fernando Gomez-Pinilla, a neurosurgery and physiological science professor at the University of California, Los Angeles, says that food is like a pharmaceutical compound that affects our brains (qtd. in Wolpert 2008). It has the ability to influence our brain health, mental function, and ability to learn and remember more efficiently.

This chapter will show you how certain food groups can do incredible things for your brain — you'll find yourself sleeping better, seeing better, and even fighting off those migraines that seem to hit during finals week.

Vegetables

At some point in your life, everyone from your mom to your doctor has probably told you to eat your vegetables. Long story short: they're right. Vegetables not only provide essential nutrients to your body, but they can also help improve your memory and concentration. The following vegetables are easy to grab, and they pair well with other healthy snacks to munch on while you study.

Leafy greens

Leafy greens improve memory and concentration. Kale, spinach, and broccoli are a few examples. Greens not only help improve the overall cognitive function of your brain, but they're high in Vitamin A and C. They're also fat-free and can help reduce risks of heart disease and cancer.

Carrots

Carrots improve eyesight and boost the immune system. In college, you're exposed to many different people every day, which means it's likely that you'll catch the flu or a cold at least once. According to researchers at Organic Facts, an informational website about healthy foods and their benefits, carrots can boost your immune system. These root-based vegetables can improve your body's ability to fight off viruses. These orange veggies can also improve your overall vision at night.

Celery

Celery calms nerves and acts as a migraine relief. It seems like everything has the ability to make you nervous and give you a headaches while you're in college. Organic Facts researchers say that eating celery can help reduce both issues. The water-based vegetable contains coumarin, a fragranced organic chemical that helps reduce pressure in the brain. High calcium levels also help calm down the nervous system in our bodies.

Fruits

Fruits also help with preserving and improving memory function. Fruits are sources of natural sugar, fiber, and antioxidants, which help stimulate the brain. According to Daniel Wallen, a health writer for **www.lifehack.org**, the brain will perform better if it's fueled by healthy fats, fiber, proteins, vitamins, and antioxidants, which all can be found in certain types of fruits.

The fruits below are easy to find in grocery stores and are healthy snack choices to bring to class or the library.

Avocados

Avocados are heart-healthy. Overall, avocados are a great source of vitamins and minerals, and they don't contain any sodium or cholesterol. These fruits contain a high amount of monounsaturated fat and folic acid that help regulate blood flow within the body. Avocados can also boost your energy levels.

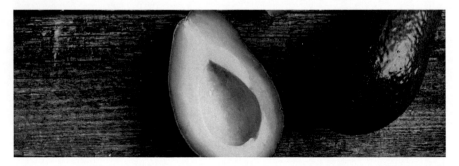

Berries

Berries help cognitive function and improve sleep. Michael Greger, M.D., says that berries contain high levels of antioxidants, which reduces health risks like cancer (2016). Antioxidants also help treat seasonal allergies and asthma. Dark berries, such as blueberries, blackberries, and cherries protect natural effects on the brain. They can delay cognitive memory loss and improve sleep schedules. If there ever were a time to stock up on the berries, it would be now.

Tomatoes and bananas

Tomatoes and bananas have high levels of potassium and iron. These nutrients are good energy boosters that you may need throughout the day. These chemicals also help maintain nerves within the body, which helps keep a normal blood flow.

Whole Grains

This food group can be tricky. Due to the popularity in fad diets, whole grains are sometimes cut out. The Whole Grain Council explains that while it may be fine to avoid whole grains for some time, it's not a good idea to avoid them forever. They have multiple health benefits, which include lowering diabetes and protecting your brain from declining cognitively, which is similar to vegetables and fruits (2016).

According to a study published by the Journal of the American College of Nutrition (2015), elementary students who ate whole grains for breakfast — or breakfast at all for that matter — scored better on standardized tests that year. College is compromised of exams and important standardized tests, so adding some whole grains to your breakfast menu may benefit your tests scores.

Here are some breakfast ideas that will incorporate whole grains into your morning routine.

Whole grain toast

Whole grain toast helps you feel full. More than often, that banana or scrambled egg in the morning isn't enough to stave off the hunger. Adding a piece or two of whole grain toast can make you feel more full throughout the day. On a side note, if you need to eat gluten-free, there are brands out there that produce gluten-free whole grain breads, so you can still benefit from whole grain nutrients.

Oatmeal

Oatmeal is good for the heart. Like most healthy foods, oatmeal is great source of protein and vitamins. It's known to reduce cholesterol levels, which keeps us heart-healthy. However, the American Cancer Society suggests eating plain, regular oats instead of the processed options, because those are full of processed sugars.

Omega-3 Fatty Acids

It doesn't sound appealing, but foods that are high in omega-3 fatty acids are said to be the healthiest types of foods to eat. They're commonly referred to as "brain-power" foods. Seafood, nuts, and foods that are high in protein like eggs and peanut butter are great examples. Here are some options.

Salmon

Salmon reduces depression. The brain is 60 percent fat, which is mostly made up of the omega-3 fatty acid chemical. Salmon, among other seafood, is very high in omega-3 fatty acids, and nutritionist Julie Daniluk says that by eating these foods, the risk of being depressed or bi-polar is reduced significantly (2016).

Walnuts

Walnuts help improve thought process, which will improve the way you learn and retain information. A handful of walnuts before class or a quiz may be just the right snack to get your brain functioning correctly!

Now that you know the health benefits attached to your daily meals, you can improve your overall ability to learn and retain information, test and sleep better, and improve the overall health of your body and brain.

So, how do you take these ingredients and incorporate them into your life? The next two chapters will show you how to eat and cook well — the fast and easy way.

CASE STUDY: EVE KECSKES, MS, RD

Nutrition by Eve, LLC
303 5th Avenue Suite 603
New York, NY 10016
www.nutritionbyeve.com
eve@nutritionbyeve.com

Eve Kecskes is a registered dietician who believes strongly that college students should incorporate daily activity into their lives. Her top ideas include going to the gym and working out with friends, going for a swim in the pool, running around the track, playing basketball, or joining a sport.

She encourages at least seven hours of sleep each night and never skipping meals. Kecskes would like to see healthy cooking clubs started on campuses or resident assistants being trained in healthy cooking to assist freshmen in getting together weekly for a healthy meal. She also suggests a column in the college newspaper devoted to healthy eating tips and sample recipes. Her nutritional advice for college students includes:

1. Try to look for lower-fat options when you have the choice.

   - Grilled chicken instead of fried chicken/chicken tenders

   - Baked potato instead of French fries

   - Pita chips instead of potato chips

   - Mustard instead of mayo

   - Veggie pizza instead of pepperoni pizza

   - Low-fat salad dressing instead of full-fat

   - Marinara sauce instead of vodka or Alfredo sauce

   - Low-fat cheese instead of full-fat

   - Turkey, chicken, ham, or fish instead of hamburgers, sausage, pepperoni, salami, bacon, or steak.

2. Start learning about portion sizes, and cut back.

   - When you buy a packaged food, look at the label and see what consists of a serving. It is easy to overdo it on crackers, cookies, candy, chips, and other foods that have multiple servings in a box/bag.

   - Cut back on portions of carbohydrates, such as bread, pasta, rice, and potatoes. While these foods are naturally low in fat, the calories add up quickly.

   - A normal dinner plate should consist of:

     - ½ fruits and vegetables

     - Lean protein

     - ¼ carbohydrates

3. There are many more suggestions that should be made as well:

   - Choose whole grains, such as oatmeal, high-fiber cereal, brown rice, whole-wheat pasta, whole-wheat bread, and popcorn, when given the option.

   - Always eat breakfast. Incorporate one of each of the following:

     - Low-fat dairy (skim or 1 percent milk, nonfat yogurt, low-fat cheese, or low-fat cottage cheese)

     - Fruit (one cup)

     - Whole grains (whole-wheat bread/English muffin/bagel, high-fiber cereal, or oatmeal)

   - Choose unsaturated fats instead of saturated/trans fats.

     - Unsaturated (vegetable oil, nuts/seeds, fatty fish, avocado, and olives)

     - Saturated (butter, whole fat dairy, red meat, poultry skin, cheese, cream, coconut, and palm oil)

     - Trans fat (partially hydrogenated oil)

- Limit sugar intake.

  - Added sugars should be no more than 10 percent of daily caloric intake

  - Fruit should be eaten for sweets instead of candy and cookies

- Drink at least eight glasses of water each day; limit sugary drinks such as sweetened coffee, soda, and juice.

- Do not overdo caffeine.

  - Energy drinks should not be used to stay up late.

  - Limit coffee and other caffeinated drinks to two per day.

4. Eat at least one vegetable or one fruit with each meal and snack.

Kecskes (formerly Salik) is the president of Nutrition by Eve, LLC, a private nutrition practice located in Manhattan. She is a registered dietitian (RD) with the American Dietetic Association who uses an individualized approach based on lifestyle, eating habits, and nutritional goals to achieve optimal health and well being. She specializes in disease prevention and management, weight loss, sports nutrition, pre- and post-natal nutrition, and general wellness.

CHAPTER 7

The Fast and Easy Way to Eat Well

The entire process of preparing and cooking a meal can be too time consuming, especially when you have class, homework, a possible part-time (or full time, for that matter) job, and a social life.

That's where all of these tips come in. There are a ton of different tools you can use to make sure you're spending your time well. From meal prep to cooking in bulk, this chapter will save you loads of precious time.

Meal Prep

Making a grocery list, actually going to the grocery store, and then coming home to prep and cook a meal? We don't have time for that. That's where meal prep comes in (or Meal Prep Monday if you're in tune with social media). Here are five easy ways to meal prep in order to make your life way easier.

Tip # 1: Marinade your meat as soon as you get home from the grocery store.

If you season or marinade your meat as soon as you get home, you can put it in freezer bags and designate them to the freezer or fridge (depending on how soon you plan on cooking it). That way, when you're ready to cook a meal, you can just grab a pre-portioned baggie and throw it in a pan. No portioning, marinating, or seasoning hassles for you.

Tip #2: Hard-boil your eggs.

Nothing is easier than grabbing an egg on your way out the door. Here's how you do it:

- Put the eggs in a pot and cover with 1 inch of cold water.

- Bring the eggs to a boil over medium-high heat, then cover, remove from the heat, and set aside for 8 to 10 minutes.
- Drain and cool them in iced water.

Tip #3: Cut veggies in bulk.

It's way easier to cut up a huge batch of zucchini and squash all at once than it is to cut small batches every day. When you get home from the grocery store, or when you find yourself with a little extra time, pre-cut your veggies for the week and put them in baggies. If you do this, your dinner can be as easy as grabbing that bag of marinated meat and that bag of pre-cut veggies and tossing them in a pan.

Tip #4: Divvy up your snacks.

How many times have you grabbed a full bag of potato chips and then realized 20 minutes later that your hand was scraping the bottom? If you divvy up your snacks into pre-portioned containers, you won't only be saving your waistline, but you'll be saving time and money.

Tip #5: Bake your breakfast in muffin tins.

You want a hot breakfast every morning, but you're flying out the door five minutes late? No worries, try baking breakfast muffins up to five days in advance. Visit the daily burn (**http://dailyburn.com/life/recipes/egg-muffins-breakfast-recipes**) for a variety of breakfast muffin recipes. You can also make these and freeze them.

There are many different ways you can meal prep — most people do this on Sundays so that they don't have to worry about it during the work/

school week. If you can, try to set aside some time on Sunday night to plan out your meals for the week. You'll be thanking yourself later.

The Art of the Crock-Pot

If you don't already have one, you're going to want one by the end of this section.

Crock-pots are a college student's best friend, because you just put the ingredients in the thing and go on with your life. When you come home at the end of your busy day, all you have to do is take off the lid and chow down.

There's really no technique to using to a crock-pot. All you need are some handy recipes, so here are three to get you started, courtesy BodyBuilding.com. There are free recipes all over the Web, so odds are, you can search your go-to meal, and there will be a crock-pot recipe for it.

1) Salsa Chicken: Throw 4 lbs. of boneless, skinless chicken breasts into a crockpot. Toss in a 16 oz. jar of salsa (check the ingredients list for added sugars). Finally, add in a 28 oz. jar of no-sodium diced tomatoes. That's it. If you need it in 3-4 hours, cook on high. If you need it in 6-7 hours, cook on low.

2) Split Pea Soup (Vegan): Add all of these ingredients to your crock-pot and cook it on low for 12-14 hours. You might need to check it every 4 hours or so to see if it needs more water.

- 1 Cup Green Split Peas (pre-soaked overnight)
- 1 Chopped White Onion

- 1 Sliced Carrot
- 2 Sliced Celery Sticks
- 3 tbsp. Liquid Aminos
- 1 tsp. Cumin
- Any blend of seasonings you like (make sure there is no added sugar)
- 8-10 Cups of Water

3) The College Boy: You need not do any preparation at all. Place 4 boneless chicken breasts at the bottom of the crockpot (thawed or frozen). Add a can of drained black beans. Add a can of drained corn. Throw some salsa on top. Cook for 7-8 hours on low or 4-5 hours on high. You can melt some cream cheese on top when it's done. That's it. Enjoy.

Freezing

Freezing food really goes hand-in-hand with meal prep. If you buy chicken in bulk, you can then break it down by chopping it up and seasoning/marinating it. Then, you can put portions into freezer baggies and save it for when you need it. Pull out the bag the night before you're going to cook it, and you just cut down your cooking time.

You don't have to do this for only chicken, though chicken is the most practical ingredient to do this with. You can buy a huge bag of frozen broccoli, which is already pre-cut and cooked for you. It'll save you money and time, and you won't have to worry about it going bad before you have a chance to cook it. Keep in mind that a lot of frozen vegetables are paired with added sugars. Always check the ingredients list before you make the purchase.

There are some ingredients that freeze really poorly. These include the following:

- Lettuce
- Cucumbers
- Bean sprouts
- Raw potatoes
- Hard boiled eggs
- Mayonnaise
- Any dairy products

Always use bags that are labeled as "freezer safe," and try to squeeze out as much air as you can from the bag. You can also use plastic tupperware as long as you seal the lid really well.

Also, you can freeze an entire meal, or you can opt to freeze individual ingredients. No matter what you decide, freezing is sure to save you some time and energy during your busy school week.

Cooking in Bulk

Cooking in bulk pairs up really well with meal prepping and freezing. If you're going to spend the time to cook a chicken breast, why not cook four at a time so that you don't have to later?

The idea of bulk cooking is to spend about 1-2 hours on one day cooking your meals for the next seven days. In other words, you're cooking for 1-2 hours out of your 168-hour week. That's not that big of a commitment.

This concept could save you so much money — instead of going out to eat, you're more likely to eat your already prepared food. You can also buy your ingredients in bulk, which usually snags you a deal. It'll keep you healthier, too.

The most important thing to do when cooking in bulk is to keep your food as naked as possible. When I say "naked," I mean don't add any sauces or seasonings to it. When you're ready to heat your food up, then you can go ahead and add in the fun by topping it off with dips, fresh seasonings, dressings, or sauces.

For example, if you cook a huge batch of brown rice on Sunday, you can stick it in the fridge and use it throughout the week in different ways. You can add it to your sauté pan for fried rice, you can add it to a burrito, you can use it as your base for chicken and veggies, or whatever else you come up with.

There are tons of helpful websites out there that have awesome bulk recipes. You can start out slow by just doing a single meal, or you can go all in and cook every meal for your entire week in one sitting. Do a little searching on the Web and find some recipes that speak to you.

Healthy On the Go Options

When you're walking out the door, the easiest thing to do is to grab something and go. With protein bars in the grocery store containing over 400 calories and up to 27 grams of sugar, you need a better, healthier option. Here are some healthy on the go options that'll keep your cravings to the minimum.

1) Whole wheat crackers with peanut butter

Nothing is easier than buying a bag of whole-wheat crackers and a jar of peanut butter. If you pre-portion your crackers and peanut butter, all you have to do is grab some baggies and head out the door. If you're really falling behind, grab the box and jar and be on your way. We won't judge.

2) Any kind of fruit

Fruit is arguably the easiest healthy snack to eat on the go. All you have to do is pick it up and leave.

3) Nuts

If you buy a bigger bag of your favorite kind of nut (we like almonds and walnuts), you can pre-portion it for quick snacking. Even if you didn't pre-portion, it only takes five seconds to grab a handful and throw it in a bag. Make sure to read the ingredient label before buying for added sugars. The best way to go is raw and unsalted.

4) Protein bars

These are trickier to purchase because of the misleading assortment in the grocery aisle. Many protein bars are also very high in sugar, which make the whole point of eating the snack useless. However, all is not lost. If you don't want to make your own protein bars at home, the brands KIND and LaraBar have some of the best options.

5) Veggies with dip

You can pre-cut some of your favorite veggies (we like celery, carrots, broccoli, and cherry tomatoes) so that you can just grab a bag and go. Browse the grocery aisle for a health-friendly dip to pair with your veggies. Just watch out for added sugars.

You can get creative with your fast and easy ways of eating. Don't let us stop you here — the Web has tons of fun and interesting content to look through. We promise you won't go hungry.

CASE STUDY: AUDREY A. KOLTUN, RD, CDE, CDN

askoltun@hotmail.com

CLASSIFIED CASE STUDIES

Koltun is a registered dietician, and she believes time management is a paramount concern for college students — especially making time for regular meals, including breakfast. She states: "Even a quick bite in the morning is very beneficial for energy and academic achievement, and it helps prevent overeating later in the day from increased hunger. Eating a meal or a healthy snack every four to five hours is important."

Koltun reminds us to schedule time for physical activity and to be conscientious of food portion sizes. She would like to see nutrition information be given as part of college orientation and also suggests "taste tests" to encourage healthy eating in the dining hall. Her top advice to students includes:

1. Try to eat fruits and vegetables every day, and try to consume plenty of water.

2. Do not linger in the dining hall. The longer you are there, the more you will eat.

3. Keep healthy snacks handy — in the dorm and with you in class. This can prevent overeating by avoiding extreme hunger when you are not eating for extended periods of time.

Koltun works in the New York metropolitan area providing nutrition counseling to clients of all ages, from children and adolescents to adults. She provides medical nutrition therapy in various areas, including weight management, type I and type II diabetes, cardiovascular nutrition, and general nutrition and wellness. Koltun also does workshops and lectures on matters relating to nutrition and health.

CHAPTER 8

—❶-❶-❶—

Cooking Basics

If you're going to stop ordering take out, you're going to have to learn how to cook. Hopefully you've picked up some basic skills along the line, but if you haven't the slightest clue, here are some cooking fundamentals.

One of the most important things about switching to a healthier diet is learning how to cook. We strongly encourage you to hop on the Web and learn as much as you can. Start small with a good-sounding recipe, and go from there. A casual evening watching the Food Network doesn't hurt, either.

Breakfast

Breakfast is a fun, simple meal to fix. It's best to begin learning to cook the things you love, and then you can start experimenting — if you want to get really into it, we love this Coconut Pancake recipe from Paleo Hacks: **http://blog.paleohacks.com/coconut-flour-pancakes/#.**

Eggs

Eggs can be fried, scrambled, or boiled. Since we already taught you how to boil eggs, here are some guidelines for frying and scrambling.

To fry eggs, use a small skillet. You can use cooking oil spray or a teaspoon of oil or butter to begin. Swirl the oil or margarine to coat the plan, carefully crack the egg, and open it with both hands to avoid breaking the yolk. This takes practice. Place one or two eggs in the skillet, and allow them to cook. Add salt or pepper if you'd like. For sunny side up, place a lid on the skillet, and turn the heat down to medium low until the yolk is set. For regular fried eggs, turn them over with a spatula as soon as you are able to. Cook to desired doneness, and remove with the spatula.

Scrambled eggs can be made many different ways. If you like fluffy eggs, crack one or two eggs, and place them in a mixing bowl. Add up to one tablespoon of milk per egg. Some people add a few drops of water instead, and some add nothing. Add salt or pepper if you want. Beat it with a fork, or whip it until it looks consistent. In the meantime, prepare a skillet with spray, oil, or butter, as done with the fried eggs. Add the scrambled egg mixture to the skillet with the heat set to medium. Stir with a spoon or spatula until it's cooked all the way through.

Bacon

The simplest bacon is the kind that is already cooked, allowing you to just heat it in the microwave. Do the math, and see how many slices you get for what price; you may be surprised to see that cooked bacon is sometimes the more economical choice.

If you decide to cook bacon from scratch, one way to fix it is in the oven. Turn your oven to 400 degrees and place the slices of bacon, barely touching or not touching at all, on a 9x13 inch pan or on a cookie sheet with raised edges. Place in the oven on the top rack. Watch it closely, and turn after it begins to get done — usually five to ten minutes.

Bacon can also be placed in a cold, large skillet and cooked on medium (you don't need to oil the pan first). You may wish to cut the slices in two before placing them in the skillet. They will need to be turned at least once. A griddle set on medium is also an excellent place to cook bacon. Place the cooked bacon on a paper towel to allow the excess grease to be absorbed.

You can also branch out and try different types of bacon, like turkey bacon.

Sausage

Sausage may be purchased raw or already cooked.

Raw sausage comes in a plastic wrapper and must be used fairly quickly or frozen once it has been opened. Remove what you want from the wrapper, and cut it into the amount of slices you wish. It is best not to cut it too thick; about a third of an inch is perfect. Alternatively, if it begins to make a mess when you try to cut it, feel free to shape it like a small, thin hamburger patty.

Use a cold skillet (or the griddle) and spray with the cooking oil spray if it is not a nonstick surface. Cook it on medium, turning at least three times with a fork or plastic spatula, until it's well done.

If you are preparing links or patties that are already cooked, follow the label instructions carefully, as they will vary quite a bit.

Oatmeal

There are three basic kinds of oatmeal: instant, quick, and old-fashioned.

For instant oats, follow the directions, which will generally entail boiling a small amount of water in a saucepan or the microwave and adding it to a bowl with the oatmeal. Stir well, and allow it to sit for a minute.

For quick oatmeal, add a little over one cup of water to a saucepan and heat on medium-high until it's boiling. Add ½ cup of oats, and stir frequently until they are the consistency that you like.

For old-fashioned oats, add 1¼ cups of water to a saucepan and heat on medium-high until boiling. Add ½ cup of oats, and turn down the head to medium-low. Stir frequently and cook for five minutes or longer. For all types of oatmeal other than flavored, put in your favorite additions after putting the oatmeal in the bowl. You can add cinnamon, honey, berries, walnuts, pecans, and any other flavors you think of.

Lunch

One of the easiest things to make for lunch is salad. You don't really need to know how to cook when it comes to salad — shop for your favorite type of greens (spinach, kale, romaine lettuce, a mixture) and top it with whatever you want (walnuts, dried cranberries, feta cheese, tomatoes, carrots). When choosing a salad dressing, always check the ingredients list for added sugars and processed oils. We love Opa salad dressings, which use Greek yogurt as the base instead of hydrogenated oils.

If you like sandwiches, be sure to use whole grain breads. Other than that, you can build up your dream sandwich with whatever ingredients you love. Expert tip: When looking for deli meat, search for the label "No Nitrates" or "No Added Nitrates."

Soup is another popular lunch item. Whether canned or homemade, it provides nourishment and helps you to feel full. Opt for soups that are broth-based instead of cream-based. Watch out for loads of sodium.

Dinner

Dinner strikes fear in the heart of many a beginner cook. It can be intimidating, but don't worry. If you can master some basic cooking techniques, you should be able to take any recipe and ace it.

Roasted chicken

Buy a whole chicken. Rub it down with your favorite spices. If you have no clue what spices you like, pick up a spice mix (we love Mrs. Dash). Preheat your oven to 500 degrees. Place your seasoned chicken on a roasting pan, breast side up, on one of the upper oven racks.

Loosely tie the legs together with kitchen twine and tuck the wing tips under. Brush the chicken all over with some butter (we love Kerrygold). Pour one cup of water into the roasting pan.

Brush the chicken with butter every 15 minutes or so to get it crispy. After 30 minutes, reduce the oven temperature to 350°. Remove the chicken from the oven and let it rest for 15–20 minutes.

Return the chicken to the oven and let it roast until the skin is golden brown and a thermometer inserted into the thickest part of the thigh registers 165°; this will take about 40–45 minutes.

Seared chicken

If you don't have time for all that, throwing some chicken into a pan can be a lot easier and less time consuming.

Put enough oil or butter into a frying pan to generously coat the bottom. Heat the pan on the stovetop over medium heat until the oil simmers — this takes about three minutes. Place your marinated or seasoned chicken breasts in the pan. Don't move the chicken around, because a nice golden-brown crust is forming.

After about six to seven minutes, flip the chicken using a metal spatula or tongs. (If the chicken sticks to the pan, it's not ready to be flipped yet. Wait about one more minute and then it should release, but don't force it.) Cook the second side for about six to seven minutes.

Check the thickest part of the breasts with a meat thermometer — you're looking for it read 160 to 165 degrees Fahrenheit.

If you dice the chicken up into smaller pieces, it won't take this long.

Pasta

To channel your inner chef, you're going to try to cook your pasta "al-dente," which basically means firm and not soggy. Fill a pan with double the water to cover the pasta, add some salt, and bring it to a boil.

Drop the pasta into the boiling water and cook it for 10-12 minutes, making sure to stir it within the first two minutes to prevent sticking. Different types of pasta will have different cooking instructions, so always read the label.

From there, you can add whatever meat you want, whatever veggies you like, and whatever sauce is your favorite. When buying a sauce, check that ingredient list. Your meal can go from hot tamale to garbage status real quick.

Rice

Luckily for you, this staple food item has easy instructions on the back. We'll include a general guideline, but you should be good to go with the packaging.

Brown rice takes longer to cook than white rice. To properly cook it on the stove, you put the brown rice and water together in a pot with a lid. Use the ratio of 1.5 cups water to 1 cup rice.

Set the heat to high, and bring the mixture to a boil (uncovered). Then, put the lid on the pot, and reduce the heat to low. Let the rice simmer for 20 minutes.

Turn off the heat and let the rice sit in the covered pot for another 10 minutes. It's fine if you let the rice sit longer than 10 minutes, but don't let it go any less.

Vegetables

If you buy vegetables frozen, they're already cooked. All you need to do is throw them in a pan with some water and let them heat up. You can do the same thing in the microwave.

If you buy fresh veggies and want to steam them, you can either buy a steamer or you can put them in a pan with some water. Here are some cooking time guidelines:

Broccoli	10-12 minutes
Asparagus	5-10 minutes
Carrots	5-15 minutes
Cauliflower	10-12 minutes
Green beans	20-30 minutes
Potatoes	15-25 minutes

If you buy veggies that are better for stir-fry, it's pretty easy. Put the firmer veggies in the oiled-up pan first (onions and bell peppers). Let them cook for a few minutes, and then add in softer veggies (zucchini, garlic, broccoli, corn). Let those cook for a little bit and add in whatever sauce you want as well as any kind of pasta or rice. It's super easy. Just make sure you put the firmer veggies on the pan first. There are tons of stir-fry recipes out there, so give one a shot!

These are just some starter tips — start here and branch out. Research recipes online; there are free recipes nearly everywhere. Once you start trying, you'll slowly get the hang of it. Don't let one botched attempt get you down — I know I've screwed up a recipe more than once — let it be a learning lesson. You might have to order take-out after all that night, but don't give up.

CHAPTER 9

⟨-⟨-⟨

Understanding Alcohol

Many students start to drink alcohol during their college years. It tends to be for one of two reasons. The first reason is the desire to party — to be in an altered state of mind. The second is to deal with the stress of adult life and college studies. You have to decide for yourself whether these are good reasons to consume alcohol.

Consider these facts:

- Some people are more at risk of becoming addicted. With genetic predisposition to alcoholism, you could spend a good part of your life as an alcoholic, which is all-consuming and life ruining.
- People often do activities they regret while under the influence of alcohol; think of driving under the influence, being in a bad social situation (such as date rape), or being in a video that forever haunts you.

If you are of legal age and do consume alcohol, it is best not to over-consume. Alcohol contains empty calories and can cause you to rob your body of essential nutrients, leaving you fatigued, stressed, and with a weakened immune system.

Beyond all of this, drinking alcohol during college brings up some daunting statistics.

Statistics on College Drinking

All of the following statistics are courtesy the National Institute on Alcohol Abuse and Alcoholism (NIAAA) as of December 2015.

- About four out of every five college students drinks alcohol.
- About half of those who do drink binge drink.

With this in mind, let's look at some of the statistics that range from academic problems to death.

- About 25 percent of college drinks report academic problems. These include: missing class, falling behind, doing poorly on exams or papers, and receiving lower grades overall.
- 599,000 students are unintentionally injured while under the influence.
- More than 97,000 students are sexually assaulted or raped while under the influence.
- More than 150,000 students develop an alcohol-related health problem and between 1.2 and 1.5 percent of students say they tried to commit suicide within the past year due to drinking or drug use.
- More than 690,000 students are assaulted by another student who has been drinking.
- 1,825 college students die each year from alcohol-related injuries.

The numbers on your overall quality of life are astounding. Even mentioning the negative health benefits seems shallow when you think about what can happen to you as a whole, but they are there, too.

Effects of Excessive Alcohol on the Body

Alcohol's negative effect on your body is really disheartening. You can experience damage to your brain, heart, liver, and pancreas as well as an increased risk of certain types of cancer. Your immune system also weakens, making it much easier to catch diseases.

Here is a list of the possible outcomes:

- Brain damage — mood changes, difficulty thinking clearly, and coordination issues
- Cardiomyopathy — stretching and drooping of the heart muscle
- Arrhythmias — irregular heart beat
- Stroke
- High blood pressure
- Steatosis, or fatty liver
- Alcoholic hepatitis
- Fibrosis
- Cirrhosis
- Mouth cancer
- Esophagus cancer
- Throat cancer
- Liver cancer
- Breast cancer
- Weak immune system

These are just the physical issues that excessive drinking can cause. When you drink alcohol, you're consuming calories, and it's usually in the form of sugar. You can expect to pack on the pounds when you're slurping down those tropical mixed drinks and heavier craft beers.

If all of that isn't enough, excessive drinking will lead to vomiting and headaches. If you've experienced a hangover, you're well aware of the pain and suffering that comes after a night of binge drinking.

How Much is Too Much

Since studies show that four out of every five college student drinks, it's safe to say that it's somewhat expected. Though drinking under the age of 21 is illegal, if students are going to do it anyway, it's important to educate them on how much is too much.

Binge drinking, the kind of drinking that leads to some pretty deadly outcomes, is defined as drinking five or more drinks in a row for men, and four or more for women.

To get more specific, we have to address not only how much is too much for a single day, but also how much is too much in general. If you go out and binge drink one time in your life, yes, there will be negative consequences, but many would agree that you don't have a problem.

According to NIAAA, "at risk" drinking is when:

- Men drink more than 14 drinks per week
- Women drink more than 7 drinks per week

To give you a better of idea of what the consequences are of drinking too often, here's a chart:

1 heavy drinking day per month	20 percent of these people have an alcohol use disorder
1 heavy drinking day per week	30 percent of these people have an alcohol use disorder
2 or more heavy drinking days per week	50 percent of these people have an alcohol use disorder

Basically, the more you drink and the more often you do it, the greater your chances are of letting it take over your life. And that's not even addressing the possible beer gut.

There is nothing wrong with going to a bar and having a cocktail or two with a friend, but be mindful about what you're drinking and how often you're doing it.

Drinking Mindfully

So, if you are going to drink, you should definitely keep your waistline in mind.

The worst thing you can drink is alcohol with sugary mixers. Avoid it by drinking liquor neat or on the rocks, or by mixing it with water, club soda, or a diet soda. Add a lemon or lime to jazz it up.

If you're feeling classy, reach for a glass of red wine. Studies have shown that red wine can have positive effects on your heart. Try to steer clear of white wine, though. It's packed full of sugary carbs.

If you love beer, you're out of luck. Almost all beer is full of carbs and is high in calories. If you can stand it, opt for a low-calorie option such as Michelob Ultra.

Remember to stay hydrated, and eat food throughout your night. Even when your liquor is mixed with water, it still isn't going to keep you fully hydrated. Count your drinks, and try to stay under the "at risk" cap.

CASE STUDY: TOBY AMIDOR, MS, RD, CDN

Food, Nutrition, and Food Safety
Consultant
E-mail: toby@namsko.com
Telephone: 914-588-0363

Registered dietician Toby Amidor feels that one of the biggest challenges to new college students involves keeping new hours. She advises to avoid late-night unhealthy eating. Amidor likes the idea of students getting together and learning how to cook. Her top three pieces of nutrition advice for college students include:

1. Schedule regular exercise. Regular exercise is also lost in the chaos of college life. Most campuses have a free gym that students can work out in and even offer classes like yoga and aerobics. Find a workout buddy, and make yourself a schedule to go to the gym. Gym classes are also offered — sign up for the ones that make you sweat, like dance and weight training.

2. Drink responsibly. It is no fun waking up after a night of heavy partying knowing you have a hangover; plus, you downed hundreds, if not thousands, of calories. Drinking tips include:

   - Stick to light beer or wine.

   - Rotate one drink and then one glass of water or a non-caloric beverage (i.e., diet soda).

   - Forget those mixed drinks — they are laden with sugar and spiked with extra alcohol to get people more drunk.

   - Forgo the "drunk pizza" at 5 a.m., and have a snack ready and waiting at home (e.g., a peanut butter and jelly sandwich).

3. Scout out all the eateries and find your quiet corner. To avoid the pressure of eating fatty foods in groups, find a nice, quiet cafeteria (or go at the off-peak hours). In my college years, I found a beautiful cafeteria that faculty went to on the other side

of campus. Take time to choose the healthiest options for you without worrying about what others will think.

Toby Amidor is a registered dietitian with a master's degree in clinical nutrition and dietetics from New York University. She is also a Certified Dietitian Nutritionist by the state of New York. Amidor is pursuing her doctoral degree in nutrition education from Teachers College — Columbia University. Amidor consults for various food-marketing and food-safety companies. Clients include Scripps Networks subsidiaries Food Network®, HGTV®, and Fine Living™. She has appeared in a variety of media outlets, including Good Day New York (WNYW Fox5 NY), Self Magazine, Us Weekly® Magazine, WebMD®, Working Mother® Magazine, The New York Daily News, and Fitness Magazine.

CHAPTER 10

The Beginner's Guide to Exercise

While this book is focused on nutrition, we'd be a little crazy to not even mention a great diet's soulmate — exercise. We won't go into a ton of detail, but we will cover the most interesting topics, including what you can expect to gain, how much of a difference it makes, and how much you should actually do it.

Benefits of Exercise

We all know that exercise is good for us, right? It's no secret that you can expect to lose weight, live longer, and be less likely to encounter a weight-related disease. But do we really understand the benefits that exercise gives us? I have a feeling that everyone would be exercising if they realized all the benefits that come along with it.

Better looking skin

A clean diet also has this effect, so imagine what your skin could look like if you combined a healthy diet with regular exercise. Physical activity boosts the circulation of nutrients to your skin, which gets rid of all the toxins.

Your skin will start getting more oxygen, which ends up producing more collagen, which makes your skin glow. It's a wonderful little domino effect.

Less stress

You're already super stressed. If you ever needed anything at this point in your life, it's exercise. The physical exertion reduces the amount of stress hormones in your body. Before long, you'll start noticing a slower heart rate and lower blood pressure.

Better mood

Is your roommate about fed up with your attitude? Try going for a jog — studies show that exercise enhances your physiological fitness while also reducing the risk of depression. Not only will you benefit from the lasting effect, but when you exercise, your body produces endorphins, which is a chemical in your brain that makes you feel on top of the world. You'll notice the feeling immediately — it's your body's way of feeding you drugs.

Less likely to get a cold

When you're in college, the worst thing that can happen can be getting sick during the middle of the semester. You have a paper due, a big lecture to go to, and you have six assignments looming over your head. The last thing you need is to be stuck in bed with a pile of used tissues. Exercising boosts your immune system making it less likely that you'll get a cold. Don't overdo it, though — too much exercise has the opposite effect.

Better grades

Okay, so exercising might not be the only thing needed to get better grades, but it definitely helps. The physical activity boosts blood flow to your brain, making it easier for your brain to fire off brain waves more quickly. You'll stop lagging and losing your train of thought.

Better sleep

We don't have to say much for this one, do we? You're cramming all the time and falling asleep on top of your textbooks. This benefit is well worth it.

Why Combine Healthy Eating With Exercise?

You may be thinking something along the lines of "sure, I can eat well, but I don't see why I need to exercise, too."

We understand. It's hard to spare the time to exercise when you're so busy, and eating healthy sounds like it'd be enough. Beyond all the benefits that exercise has to offer alone, when you combine eating well with physical activity, you can eat more.

The formula is simple: calories in, calories out. You can only eat as many calories as your body burns to maintain your body weight. If you eat more calories than your body burns, you'll gain weight.

So, when you exercise, you boost how many calories your body is burning, which means that you can eat more food without gaining weight.

It's also a fabulous spiral effect, because when you exercise, your muscle mass grows. Muscle burns fat. It's a win-win.

Also, you can look thin and healthy without actually being physically fit. When you exercise, you're fueling your body from the inside out, meaning you won't only look fit, but you'll actually *be* fit.

Cardio & Weight Training

In general, doing cardio is best for fat loss, while weight training is best for muscle gain.

If your goal is to lose fat, you should focus on cardio exercises, which range on a scale from low-intensity to high-intensity. Low-intensity cardio workouts will be walking or slow cycling, while high-intensity cardio workouts will be activities like sprinting or interval training. Moderate-intensity workouts fall in the middle with activities like jogging or swimming.

Bodybuilding.com suggests doing a cardio exercise 1-2 times per week to lose fat without losing too much muscle.

Weight training can be more difficult to understand, which is where outside research and reading will come in handy. There are a ton of different exercises that fall in the realm of weight training — from good ol' squats to wide-grip lat pulldowns — to fully understand all of these exercises, we recommend that you meet up with a fitness coach to show you around the gym.

A nice afternoon Web search doesn't hurt, either.

Bodybuilding.com suggests that you train with weights about three times per week to grow your muscles without overtraining them. Once you start getting better, and your body can recover faster, you can increase that number to as high as six days per week.

Getting Started

The world of exercise is a complex and interesting one — the more you read, the more you realize how insanely good it is for your body. The same goes for actually exercising — the more you do it, the better you feel.

The easiest way for you to get started is to start out at your college or university's gym. See if they offer free classes — not only will this keep you accountable, but it's a fun way to meet new people. You can also see if they have a personal trainer that you can do a session with if you aren't so sure how to navigate your way around the gym.

Start small — you don't want to burn yourself out and dread going to the gym. If you force yourself to go for over an hour while exerting yourself so much that you can barely walk down the stairs afterwards, you might not want to go anymore. (If you can, props to you!) When you ease yourself into it, you're more likely to keep it up. Even going for a 30 minute walk each day can have dramatic effects on your health.

Don't get discouraged — you have what it takes to make it happen. We can't complain about anything in life if we don't take steps to change it.

CASE STUDY: BEN GREENFIELD, NUTRITION EXPERT AND VOTED AMERICA'S TOP PERSONAL TRAINER

In his article "Advice for New College Grads – How to Lose The Freshman 15," Ben Greenfield gives four key pieces of advice (2011).

1. **Exercise.** No matter how poor your dietary choices are, frequent physical activity will help to stave off at least some of the damage. At least 2 times per week, do "The Best Workout for Fat Loss," which involves a series of resistance training exercises, followed by a 30-60 second bout of high intensity cardio. On the days you can't squeeze in a structured session, instead try quick workouts, which you can read more about in "How to Do a 10-Minute Workout." Finally when that's not an option, try to stand whenever possible, walk or bike to your classes, and avoid sitting for long periods of time.

2. **Eat Healthy.** Rather than completely re-inventing the wheel, I am going to instead recommend that you check out two episodes from the Nutrition Diva: "Healthy Eating Tips for College Kids" and "More Healthy Eating Tips For College Kids." Both of these articles give you everything you need to know to make the right choices at the cafeteria and on a budget. In addition to these tips, try to drink high amounts of caffeine or energy drinks only when absolutely necessary, such as a series of all-nighters during finals week. If you're already out of college, able to eat healthy, and want to get rid of the Freshman 15, try rebooting your body by taking 2 months to cut down on all your college staples, such as processed food from packages, starches and refined sugars, alcohol, and caffeine.

3. **Control Stress.** While a daily yoga routine is probably going to be tough to coordinate with a busy course load, you can make small changes to control stress. During classes, practice breathing deeply through your nose, and then breathing

out through slightly pursed lips. When you feel overloaded with homework, try breaking it down into small, achievable portions. And when you experience stressful social situations, try venting to a friend, or simply in your own personal diary. Both can help you from keeping things bottled up and putting your body into stressed out, fat storage mode. If you're living a high-stress, post-collegiate life, you may actually have the time to add a weekly or bi-weekly yoga class, which I highly encourage.

4. **Optimize Sleep.** Read the House Call Doctor's great episode on getting better sleep. While you will almost never have ideal sleep patterns during busy school life, take advantage of the days that are lighter to catch up on sleep or get an extra nap, and try to avoid partying for multiple days in a row whenever possible. If you're out of college, catch up on rest and recovery by making every lifestyle change that you can to give your body a couple months of 8-hour-per-night sleep cycles, even if it means cutting out your favorite TV show or social networking time.

*Read more at **www.quickanddirtytips.com** and **www.bengreenfield fitness.com**. You can also download his app on the App Store to listen to health and wellness podcasts — "BGFitness."*

CONCLUSION

My biggest fear is that our generation is going to give up on eating healthy because we aren't sure what exactly healthy is.

The media, money, and politics make it really hard to sift through all the agenda-driven information. We don't know which article to believe, which study is actually accurate, or even what that label on our food means.

My hope is that this book will show you the importance of researching both sides of the argument — if you do a Web search for "Benefits of *something*," you'll be sure to find list after list of benefits. It's so important to take a step on the other side of the line and also search for "Disadvantages or Drawbacks of *that same thing*."

You want to be able to go into a debate knowing both sides, not just one. So, know that this book isn't trying to sway you in any direction except the truth.

Whatever you decide, know that any step in the right direction is going to help you not only avoid the Freshman 15, but it's going to give you a ton of other college-friendly benefits. Before you know it, you'll have better sleep, better focus, better skin — you name it, it's going to be better.

Take a healthy step forward and ace those exams. You've earned it.

AUTHOR'S NOTE

Nowadays, it's hard to find factual information on anything nutrition-related. Everyone seems to have an agenda. Companies want to sell more of their products, so they publish research that's in their favor. People make commission if they endorse a particular product or brand, so they talk it up.

Long story short, money drives everything.

Who do you trust? How can you sift through all the information out there? Is that fad diet really worth it, or do people just want your money?

The beauty of this book is that we don't have an agenda. We're searching for the truth, just like you. We aren't trying to sell any products, we don't make commission off of any of this material, and we don't owe anyone any favors. In this book, you see research — and not just one-sided, sponsored research. I mean research that covers every point of view.

We included debates, with each voice of the argument being presented to you, so that you can make your most informed decision on what you think is best. You see scientific research explained simply so that you don't have to waste your time sifting through material that's nearly impossible to read. You see pros and cons lists as well as case studies.

Most importantly, you see how all of this applies to you and your first year of college. What the heck is the Freshman 15 and how does it affect *you*? We teach you everything from how to decipher those long words in the ingredient list to what the difference is between white and brown rice.

The best part? Everything is explained through research and experts.

That's why we created this all-inclusive, unbiased guide to being the healthiest you've ever been for your first year of college.

Well, not just your first year.

To infinity and beyond.

APPENDIX

—❶-❶-❶—

Nutrition Calculator

If you have no idea how much of those macronutrients you should be eating every day, here are some ways for you to find out.

SELFNutritionData
(http://nutritiondata.self.com/tools/calories-burned)

This site asks you to enter your sex, your age, your weight, your height, and your lifestyle. Once you add in this information, it will not only give you your BMI, but it will tell you about how many calories you burn each day. It tells you how many carbs you should be eating as well as how much protein.

My Fitness Pal
(www.myfitnesspal.com)

This website and app make it easy to track your food intake. When you sign up, you'll fill out information for yourself, and it will give you guidelines on everything from protein intake to sugar intake. You can use the app to track exactly what you're eating so that you'll know in advance exactly how many calories are coming in and how many are going out.

FactsUpFront.org
(www.factsupfront.org/calculator)

This site also asks you to enter in your personal information. It then tells you how many calories you should eat to maintain your current weight. You'll also see numbers on fiber, protein, calcium, iron, and more.

Calorie Count
(www.caloriecount.com/tools/calories-goal)

This site asks you to enter your current weight, your goal weight, and the date you want to reach your goal weight. It will then tell you how many calories you would need to consume to reach your goal. The site recommends losing no more than 0.5 to 2 pounds per week.

BodyBuilding.com
(www.bodybuilding.com/fun/macronutrients_calculator.htm)

This calculator asks you to enter in personal details (age, sex, height, weight, etc.). Then, it spits out how many macros you should be consuming (carbs, proteins, and fats). This can be useful if you want to make sure you're consuming the right amounts of macronutrients, but remember that this is just one suggestion. You should consult several sites to get an idea of the average recommendation.

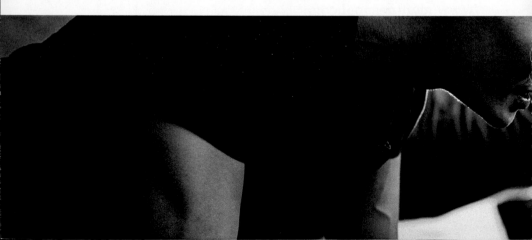

Macronutrient Calculator
(http://macronutrientcalculator.com)

This site doesn't have any real suggestion for you — it just spits out the information. You enter how many calories you plan on eating each day (which you can figure out using one of the above methods), and then you decide which kind of diet you'd like to do (High Carb, Moderate, Zone Diet, or Low Carb). Then, the system spits out how many carbs, proteins, and fats you should be eating depending on what your goal is. Keep in mind, though, that even the "Low Carb" option is nowhere near as low in carbs as a standard Ketogenic diet would be.

Keto Calculator
(http://keto-calculator.ankerl.com)

This calculator is a little more difficult to navigate through, but once you get the hang of it, you'll learn what your macro goals would be for a Ketogenic diet. Since the previous calculator didn't have that option, we wanted to be sure to include a source for those interested in this very low carb diet.

BIBLIOGRAPHY

"A Gluten Free Diet, How Much Will It Cost You?" *CBSNews*. CBS Interactive, 25 Feb. 2014. Web. 15 Apr. 2016.

"Benefits of Eating Grass Fed Beef." *Grassfed Network*. Grassfed Network, 8 July 2012. Web. 22 Apr. 2016.

"How Do Artificial Flavors Work?" *HowStuffWorks*. 31 May 2000. Web. 4 Apr. 2016.

"The Charlie Foundation for Ketogenic Therapies." *The Charlie Foundation*. 2014. Web. 15 Apr. 2016.

"The Grassfed Exchange." *The Grassfed Exchange*. The Grassfed Exchange, 11 Jan. 2016. Web. 22 Apr. 2016.

"The Paleo Diet." *The Paleo Diet*. The Paleo Diet, 2016. Web. 15 Apr. 2016.

Ace Fitness Editorial. "A Walk a Day." *American Council on Exercise*. 24 Jan. 2013. Web.

Andrews, David. "Natural vs. Artificial Flavors." *EWG's Food Scores*. Environmental Working Group. Web. 4 Apr. 2016.

Boles, Myde, Barbara Pelletier, and Wendy Lynch. "The Relationship Between Health Risks and Work Productivity." *Journal of Occupational and Environmental Medicine* 46.7 (2004): 737-45. Web.

Bostick, Roberd M., John D. Potter, Lawrence H. Kushi, Thomas A. Sellers, Kristi A. Steinmetz, David R. Mckenzie, Susan M. Gapstur, and Aaron R. Folsom. "Sugar, Meat, and Fat Intake, and Non-dietary Risk Factors for Colon Cancer Incidence in Iowa Women (United States)." *Cancer Causes & Control Cancer Causes Control* 5.1 (1994): 38-52. Web.

Brandt, Michelle. "Little Evidence of Health Benefits from Organic Foods, Study Finds." *Stanford Medicine.* Stanford University, 3 Sept. 2012. Web. 4 Apr. 2016.

Campbell, T. Colin, and Howard Jacobson. *Whole: Rethinking the Science of Nutrition.* BenBella, 2013. Print.

Campbell, T. Colin, and Thomas M. Campbell. *The China Study: The Most Comprehensive Study of Nutrition Ever Conducted and the Startling Implications for Diet, Weight Loss and Long-term Health.* Dallas, TX: BenBella, 2006. Print.

Carlton, Chris, and Kira G. Goldy. "The History of Raw Food." *Raw Food - Purely Raw, The History of Raw Food.* Purely Raw, 2009. Web. 18 Apr. 2016.

Cavazos, David A., Matthew J. Degraffenried, Shruti A. Apte, Laura W. Bowers, Kaitlin A. Whelan, and Linda A. Degraffenried. "Obesity Promotes Aerobic Glycolysis in Prostate Cancer Cells." *Nutrition and Cancer* 66.7 (2014): 1179-186. Web. 2 Apr. 2016.

Conner, Tamlin S., Kate L. Brookie, Aimee C. Richardson, and
  Maria A. Polak. "On Carrots and Curiosity: Eating Fruit and
  Vegetables Is Associated with Greater Flourishing in Daily Life."
  British Journal of Health Psychology 20.2 (2014): 413-27. Web.

Consumer Reports. "Cost of Organic Food." *Consumer Reports*.
  Consumer Reports, 19 Mar. 2015. Web. 20 Apr. 2016.

Cross, Kim. "Grass-Fed Beef versus Grain-Fed Beef." *Cooking Light*.
  Cooking Light. Web. 22 Apr. 2016.

Davila, David. "Diet, Exercise and Sleep." *National Sleep Foundation*
  (Dec. 2009). Web.

Derocha, Grace. "Is the New MyPlate Food Guide Effective?
  Dietitians Weigh In." *A Healthier Michigan*. Blue Cross Blue
  Shield of Michigan, 9 June 2011. Web. 07 Apr. 2016.

Dong, Allen, and Stephen C. Scott. "Serum Vitamin B12 and Blood
  Cell Values in Vegetarians." *Annals of Nutrition and Metabolism
  Ann Nutr Metab* 26.4 (1982): 209-16. Web. 18 Apr. 2016.

European Food Information Council. "What Is the Difference
  between Organic and Conventional Food?" *Frequently Asked
  Questions*. European Food Information Council. Web. 4 Apr.
  2016.

EWG. "EWG's Shopper's Guide to Pesticides in Produce™." *Summary*.
  Environmental Working Group, 2015. Web. 07 Apr. 2016.

Farzan, Antonia. "The Cost of Being Vegan." *The Billfold*. Medium,
  06 Nov. 2014. Web. 18 Apr. 2016.

Fitzgerald, Matt. *Diet Cults: The Surprising Fallacy at the Core of Nutrition Fads and a Guide to Healthy Eating for the Rest of Us.* New York: Pegasus LLC, 2014. Print.

Flynn, Mary M., and Andrew R. Schiff. "Economical Healthy Diets (2012): Including Lean Animal Protein Costs More Than Using Extra Virgin Olive Oil." *Journal of Hunger & Environmental Nutrition* 10.4 (2015): 467-82. Web. 18 Apr. 2016.

Forte, Enrico, and Valerie Forte. "How Much Would It Cost to Eat like a Mediterranean?" *Healthy Eating Blog Food Charts Diet Plan Menu Tips and Recipes.* MediterraneanBook.com, 2010. Web. 18 Apr. 2016.

Frazier, Karen. *Nutrition Facts: The Truth about Food.* Berkeley: Rockridge, 2015. Print.

Fuhrman, Joel. *The End of Dieting: How to Live for Life.* New York: HarperCollins, 2014. Print.

Giovannucci, Edward, Michael Pollak, Elizabeth A. Platz, Walter C. Willett, Meir J. Stampfer, Noreen Majeed, Graham A. Colditz, Frank E. Speizer, and Susan E. Hankinson. "Insulin-like Growth Factor I (IGF-I), IGF-binding Protein-3 and the Risk of Colorectal Adenoma and Cancer in the Nurses' Health Study." *Growth Hormone & IGF Research* 10 (2000). Web.

Go, A. S., D. Mozaffarian, et al. "Executive Summary: Heart Disease and Stroke Statistics--2013 Update: A Report From the American Heart Association." *Circulation* 127.1 (2013): 143-52. Web.

Gordon, Megan. "What's the Difference Between Multigrain and Whole Grain?" *The Kitchn*. The Kitchn, 9 Apr. 2014. Web. 07 Apr. 2016.

Greenfield, Ben. "Advice for New College Grads – How to Lose The Freshman 15." *Quick and Dirty Tips*. Macmillan Holdings, 4 Oct. 2011. Web. 27 Apr. 2016.

Guinan, Emer M., Elizabeth M. Connolly, and Juliette Hussey. "Exercise Training in Breast Cancer Survivors: A Review of Trials Examining Anthropometric and Obesity-related Biomarkers of Breast Cancer Risk." *Physical Therapy Reviews* 18.2 (2013): 79-89. Web.

Gunnars, Kris. "5 Reasons Why Vegan Diets May Be a Bad Idea." *Authority Nutrition*. Authority Nutrition, 26 Aug. 2013. Web. 18 Apr. 2016.

Hadrick, Troy. "Study Shows Grain Fed Beef Healthier Than Grass Fed." *Advocates for Agriculture*. Blogger, 27 May 2010. Web. 22 Apr. 2016.

Healthline Editorial Team. "5 Benefits of Healthy Habits." *Healthline* (1 Apr. 2013). Web.

Hellmich, Nanci. "Freshman 15 Drops Some Pounds." *Health and Behaivor*. USA Today, 23 Oct. 2006. Web. 02 Apr. 2016.

Lefferts, Lisa Y. "Seeing Red: Time for Action on Food Dyes." Ed. Michael F. Jacobson and Laura MacCleery. *Center for Science in the Public Interest* (2016). Web. 4 Apr. 2016.

Lin, HH, PS Tsai, SC Fang, and JF Liu. "Effect of Kiwifruit Consumption on Sleep Quality in Adults with Sleep Problems." *Asia Pacific Journal of Clinical Nutrition* 20.2 (2011): 169-74. Web.

Lipscombe, Lorraine. "Insulin, Insulin Resistance, and Cancer Associations." *Insulin Resistance and Cancer* (2011): 111-40. Web.

Magee, Elaine. "Carbohydrates: Natural Carbohydrate Foods vs. Refined Carbs." *WebMD*. WebMD, 30 Oct. 2008. Web. 07 Apr. 2016.

Mercola, Joseph. "Can the Food You Eat Affect Your Mood?" *Mercola.com.* 2 Jan. 2014. Web.

Merrill, Ray M., Steven G. Aldana, James E. Pope, David R. Anderson, Carter R. Coberley, and R. William Whitmer, And The Hero Research Stud. "Presenteeism According to Healthy Behaviors, Physical Health, and Work Environment." *Population Health Management* 15.5 (2012): 293-301. Web.

Miller, Kenneth B., W. Jeffrey Hurst, Nancy Flannigan, Boxin Ou, C. Y. Lee, Nancy Smith, and David A. Stuart. "Survey of Commercially Available Chocolate- and Cocoa-Containing Products in the United States. 2. Comparison of Flavan-3-ol Content with Nonfat Cocoa Solids, Total Polyphenols, and Percent Cacao." *Journal of Agricultural and Food Chemistry* 57.19 (2009): 9169-180. Web.

National Institute on Alcohol Abuse and Alcoholism. "College Drinking." *College Drinking.* National Institute on Alcohol Abuse and Alcoholism, Dec. 2015. Web. 22 Apr. 2016.

Newcastle University. "Organic Crop Quality." *Nafferton Ecological Farming Group.* Newcastle University, 2015. Web. 4 Apr. 2016.

Nicklett, Emily J. et al. "Fruit and Vegetable Intake, Physical Activity, and Mortality in Older Community-Dwelling Women." *Journal of the American Geriatrics Society* 60.5 (2012): 862-68. Web.

Obesity Society. "Your Weight and Diabetes." *Your Weight and Diabetes.* Obesity Society, Feb. 2015. Web. 02 Apr. 2016.

Oldways Whole Grain Council. "Definition of Whole Grains." *Definition of Whole Grains.* Oldways Whole Grain Council, May 2004. Web. 07 Apr. 2016.

Page, Kathleen A., et al. "Effects of Fructose vs Glucose on Regional Cerebral Blood Flow in Brain Regions Involved With Appetite and Reward Pathways." *Jama* 309.1 (2013): 63. Web.

Palmer, Sharon. "The Mediterranean Diet — An Up-Close Look at Its Origins in Pantelleria." *Today's Dietician* May 2013: 28. Print.

Robinson, Jo. "Health Benefits of Grass-Fed Products." *Eat Wild.* Eat Wild. Web. 22 Apr. 2016.

Runyon, Joel. "How To Eat Paleo on A Budget / Ultimate Paleo Guide." *Ultimate Paleo Guide.* An Impossible Ventures Company, 06 Feb. 2014. Web. 15 Apr. 2016.

Seely, Stephen, and David F. Horrobin. "Diet and Breast Cancer: The Possible Connection with Sugar Consumption." *Medical Hypotheses* 11.3 (1983): 319-27. Web.

Slattery, M. L., J. Benson, T. D. Berry, D. Duncan, S. L. Edwards, B. J. Caan, and J. D. Potter. "Dietary Sugar and Colon Cancer." *Food and Chemical Toxicology* 35.12 (1997): 1227. Web.

Smith, Stephen B. "Grass-Fed Vs. Grain-Fed Ground Beef — No Difference In Healthfulness." *BEEF Magazine.* BEEF Magazine, 25 Mar. 2014. Web. 22 Apr. 2016.

Stephen, Ian D., Miriam J. Law Smith, Michael R. Stirrat, and David I. Perrett. "Facial Skin Coloration Affects Perceived Health of Human Faces." *Int J Primatol International Journal of Primatology* 30.6 (2009): 845-57. Web.

Suddath, Claire. "A Brief History of Veganism." *Time.* Time, 30 Oct. 2008. Web. 18 Apr. 2016.

Super Skinny Me. "Cost of Weight Loss Diets." Super Skinny Me. Web. 15 Apr. 2016.

Surmacz, Eva, and Laszlo Otvos. "Molecular Targeting of Obesity Pathways in Cancer." *Hormone Molecular Biology and Clinical Investigation* 22.2 (2015). Web.

The Daniel Plan. *The Daniel Plan.* The Daniel Plan. Web. 18 Apr. 2016.

The Vegan Society. "Health." *The Vegan Society.* The Vegan Society. Web. 18 Apr. 2016.

U.S. Department of Health and Human Services. "Overweight and Obesity Statistics." *Health Statistics.* U.S. Department of Health and Human Services, Oct. 2012. Web. 4 Apr. 2016.

Unicef. "Micronutrients and Macronutrients." *Why Care about Nutrition?* Unicef. Web. 07 Apr. 2016.

Voss, Gretchen. "When You Lose Weight — and Gain It All Back." *Health — Diet and Nutrition*. NBC News, 6 June 2010. Web. 2 Apr. 2016.

Weight Watchers. "Success Starts Here." *Weight Watchers*. Weight Watchers International. Web. 15 Apr. 2016.

Weigle, David S. "A High-Protein Diet Induces Sustained Reductions in Appetite, Ad Libitum Caloric Intake, and Body Weight Despite Compensatory Changes in Diurnal Plasma Leptin and Ghrelin Concentrations." *The American Journal of Clinical Nutrition* 82.1 (2005): 41-48. Print.

Wongvibulsin, Shannon. "Eat Right, Drink Well, Stress Less: Stress-Reducing Foods, Herbal Supplements, and Teas." *Explore IM Integrative Medicine*. UCLA.edu. 26 Sept. 2014. Web.

Zelman, Kathleen M. "Good Fats vs. Bad Fats: Get the Skinny on Fat." *WebMD*. WebMD, 1 Nov. 2007. Web. 25 Apr. 2016.

GLOSSARY

%DV Recommendations on how much of each nutrient you should eat based on a 2,000 calorie per day diet.

Clean fifteen The fifteen types of produce that are the least likely to contain pesticides.

Dirty dozen The twelve types of produce that are the most likely to contain pesticides.

Ester An organic compound made by replacing the hydrogen of an acid by an alkyl or other organic group. Many naturally occurring fats and essential oils are esters of fatty acids.

Fructose A hexose sugar found especially in honey and fruit; humans don't produce fructose.

Glucose A simple sugar that comes from starches like potatoes; our bodies produce it and every cell on the earth has glucose in it.

Glycemic index A system that ranks foods on a scale from 1 to 100 based on their effect on blood-sugar levels.

Ketogenic A high-fat, adequate-protein, low-carbohydrate diet. The diet forces the body to burn fats rather than carbohydrates.

Ketosis A normal metabolic process that your body does to keep working when it doesn't have enough carbohydrates from food for your cells to burn for energy; your body burns fat instead of carbohydrates for fuel. As part of this process, your body produces ketones.

Macronutrient A type of food (e.g., fat, protein, carbohydrate) required in large amounts in the human diet.

Micronutrient A chemical element or substance required in trace amounts for the normal growth and development of living organisms.

Multigrain Made from more than one kind of grain.

MyPlate The current nutritional guide provided by the USDA; a food circle showing you the appropriate food groups you should be consuming.

Omega-3 A class of essential fatty acids found in fish oils, especially from salmon and other cold-water fish, that acts to lower the levels of cholesterol and LDL (low-density lipoproteins) in the blood.

Omega-6 A type of polyunsaturated fatty acid necessary for human health; the body cannot naturally make this — you must get this through food.

Organic Foods produced by methods that comply with the standards of organic farming; standards vary worldwide.

Paleo Based on the notion that for optimal health, modern humans should go back to eating real, whole unprocessed foods that are more healthful than harmful to our bodies.

Processed   An item that goes through a series of mechanical or chemical operations in order to change or preserve it.

Refined   Impurities or unwanted elements removed through processing.

Satiety   The feeling or state of being full.

Standard American Diet (SAD)   In general, the idea that most Americans spend more money on refined, processed foods than whole, natural foods.

Whole grain   A cereal grain that contains the germ, endosperm, and bran, in contrast to refined grains, which retain only the endosperm.

Whole wheat   Denoting flour or bread made from whole grains of wheat, including the husk or outer layer.

INDEX

AUTHOR BIOGRAPHY

Rebekah Sack is a nonfiction author who has written several helpful guides for the young adult and college-aged audience. Her passion for helping teens survive the roller coaster of youth translates onto each page of her books. A summa cum laude graduate of Illinois State University, she now works for Atlantic Publishing Group as the in-house editor.